CONTENTS

Introduction

When I bought my first travel trailer in 1962, I had no idea it would lead to a new way of life and a third career. But after that first summer, things changed. I knew I was born to be an RV bum, a 20th Century nomad. Fortunately, I had chosen a career with forced unemployment in the summer. We quickly discovered that traveling by trailer cost no more than staying home. Our address became Anywhere, USA and Canada.

By 1980 I had decided to take early retirement from teaching. My wife Kate reminded me that I no longer had the excuse of being too busy to write. An invitation from the editor of the leading RV magazine to submit an article was all the impetus needed. What to write about? What else but RVing?

I'm still amazed at how one thing led to another. That first article sold to "Trailer Life" has resulted in columns and features in "MotorHome," "Trails-A-Way," "Camp-Orama," "Camperways," "Southern RV," "Camp Coast to Coast," "Northeast Outdoors," "Camping Today," "American RV Traveller," "Highways" and a few others. Most of those columns and articles were on the technical aspects of RVing.

By applying my natural curiosity and engineering tendencies to RVing, I discovered that there was a lot more to successful RVing than just hooking up a trailer or climbing into a motorhome. I've tried to find answers to the simple and not so simple problems RVers face. From my own experience and from conversations and letters from others, I have realized there is a lot of bad information being given to RVers by people who should know better. I hope it isn't immodest of me to say that I've helped to clear up some of the confusion with my writing and seminars at rallies.

I continue to get a lot of letters from readers. Some of them ask questions that have already been answered. That's all right. We all want an answer to our specific problem. Some ask for copies of an article they read a couple of years ago or that a friend mentioned reading. It usually isn't feasible to send the copy they want, but it is feasible to collect those columns and publish them as a book. This book is a collection of what I thought most readers would want to keep as reference material. Some of it's new; some of it appeared earlier as magazine columns.

I love RVing. Since April 1990, an RV has been my only home. Kate and I made the decision to sell our house and travel full-time. Kate died in July 1990. I like to think that she is watching and sharing the pleasure that I continue to get from the modern nomadic life. I miss her terribly, but the wonderful people I have met in RV parks and boondocking sites have helped to make it easier. I'm convinced that RVers are the finest people on Earth. Sharing the RV life and meeting each of you through this book is another reason for its writing.

Finally, I would like to dedicate this book to Kate. Without her and her continued encouragement, I would likely never have written the first article and never have known the pleasure it has given me.

I hope you enjoy the book as much as I have.

Farlow's Laws of RV Travel

•First Law -- The power needed to get over the next hill is exactly the amount you didn't buy.

•Second Law -- The quantity of things essential to take with you will exactly fill the amount of space available.

•Third Law -- Just when you finally get all the kids loaded, one of them will have to go potty -- right now!

•Fourth Law -- Fifteen minutes down the road, the one who didn't go potty will have to go -- right now!

•Fifth Law -- When you need that jack you bought at a garage sale 10 years ago, you'll find out why it was so cheap.

•Sixth Law -- An engine always runs right when the mechanic is looking at it.

•Seventh Law -- Wherever you are, whenever you're there, the weather will be unusually hot, cold, wet, dry.

•Eighth Law -- When the salesman says, "Sure, this little baby will pull your trailer easy," it won't!

•Ninth Law -- Whatever you threw away last week, you will need desperately tomorrow.

•Tenth Law -- When you're traveling, there is no such thing as a tailwind.

•Eleventh Law -- When the fan belt breaks and you look out the window to see where you are, you won't see a garage or a telephone booth.

•Twelfth Law -- Half way up Wolf Creek Pass, you'll remember you meant to get gas back in Durango.

•Thirteenth Law -- The woman waving frantically and pointing toward the back of your RV isn't just being friendly.

•Fourteenth Law -- Just as you've finished lathering up in the shower, you will discover why the water pump was sounding funny.

•Fifteenth Law -- Under no circumstances show your mother-in-law that the sofa makes down into a bed.

•Sixteenth Law -- Lies told at the poker table or around the campfire don't count.

Chapter 1

50 Things Your Dealer Never Told You

Paid a lot of money for that new rig didn't you? But it's worth it. It came with lots of goodies, too. Things like comfortable beds, a refrigerator, range and oven, furnace, lots of storage space, maybe even air conditioning. But there's something it didn't come with, and your dealer never told you. He really couldn't, of course, because the things I'm talking about are things most dealers don't know. You see, most dealers aren't RVers; they are salespersons.

Dealers sell you your RV and show you how to get out of the lot. The rest is up to you to learn on your own. Now, experience may be an excellent teacher, but I don't see any reason why everybody should start at zero. So if you'll bear with me for a few pages I'll give you a few tips to make beginning a little easier. If any of you old-timers read this and find that I've left out something, drop me a line. I would appreciate your help.

Okay, here we go. These tips are in no special order. I've just put them down as they came to me.

1. HITCHING UP

I've scared the hell out of myself a few times by thinking about what would happen if that trailer ever came loose. I saw it happen once for my dad about 30 years ago. Once is enough. A good way to avoid that is to develop a routine for hitching up and stay with it. Once you start hitching up, don't let anything stop you until you've finished.

Here's what I do. After the tow vehicle is maneuvered into position, lower the front of the trailer until the tongue weight is solidly on the ball. Close the latch and raise the jack all the way. Put the jack pad in the van. Hook up the safety chains. Hook up the spring bars and sway control. Plug in the electrical cord to the van. Hook up the breakaway switch. Inspect everything.

2. SAFETY CHAINS

I have a friend who has towed a trailer for several years. He's an otherwise intelligent person with lots of common sense. His view of safety chains is that they are for show. He hooks his up so that if the trailer should ever come unhitched, the chains will break free and let that 4000 pounds of trailer go merrily on its way. Let me state very clearly. That is extreme irresponsibility. I hope my friend's trailer never comes loose. I hope yours doesn't, either. But in case it does, make sure your safety chains are strong and securely fastened. The one time I saw a trailer get loose, the safety chains prevented a possible disaster. There was lots of noise when the lower end of the jack began scraping. The jack was bent, but that was all.

3. SPRING BARS

Spring bars, sometimes called equalizer bars, help to take some of the weight off the rear of the tow vehicle and make everything level. Your dealer probably did this one right, but check it. After you're hooked up, stand back and look at the side of the combined rig. The tow vehicle and trailer should be level with the ground and with each other.

That's the quick way. I like to be more accurate.

Tow the rig to a level area. A parking lot is good. Unhook the trailer. Measure carefully from the ground to spots on the front and rear of the tow vehicle. Hook up the trailer and spring bars. Measure from the ground to those same spots again. The front and rear of the tow vehicle should have settled the same amount. If not, change the tension on the spring bars. For example, if the rear of the tow vehicle settled more than the front, draw the chain on the spring bars up another link and measure again.

If you can't get it to come out right, the ball may

be mounted too high or too low, or the ball mount angle may be incorrect (check your hitch's instructions about ball mount angles). Unhook again. Level the trailer front to rear. The top of the ball should be level to one-half inch higher than the top of the socket on the trailer. If it isn't and you have an adjustable ball head, make the necessary adjustments. Otherwise go back to the dealer and get a ball with the correct amount of rise.

4. CHANGING A TRAILER TIRE

I hate changing a trailer tire. Unless you have a trailer with tandem axles and independent suspension, it can be a mess. If you have tandem axles, get out your leveling blocks and move your trailer onto them so that the good tire is raised two or three inches. Run the hitch jack down on a good pad until you've got enough weight on it to be solid. Then place your jack on a solid pad and under a spot on the frame as near to the axle of the bad tire as you can get. Don't place it under the axle. Tighten up until the tire starts to rise. Using the right size lug wrench, loosen the lug nuts on the bad tire. Raise the tire until it is free of the ground and remove it. Put the spare on.

What? No spare? See if the spare from your tow vehicle will fit. It probably won't. Okay, you'll have to unhitch and go to town and get it fixed.

From the above, you'll note that you should have a lug wrench which fits the lugs of the trailer. That may be a different size from the one for your tow vehicle. You'll also need a good jack. A scissors jack is fine. A 3-ton hydraulic jack is better. And you'll need some blocks or pads. Pieces of 2 X 8 boards cut about 10 inches long are good. Carry three or four with you. It would also be good to have a spare tire and wheel for the trailer.

And check to see that all tires are the same size. I recently stopped to help a motorhome driver change a tire. He was more than chagrined to learn that the only spare was for the front end. On the rear, he had super-singles instead of duals. Tough.

5. LIGHT THE FURNACE

Light the furnace? Everybody knows how to do that, don't they. Well, if you don't have one with an electronic igniter and have tried to light it with a match or cigarette lighter with a downdraft, you may have had some problems. Every time you get your match close to the opening it blows out. What to do. Just use the sparker or lighter you use for the range. Aim the sparks into the opening and no problem. You don't have a sparker? Now you have another reason to get one.

6. HOLDING TANK SOLUTIONS

Everybody uses one. The question is what kind. More and more dumping stations are having problems from some of the non-biodegradable solutions we've been using. Some of them contain formaldehyde. Nasty stuff. This year I'm using a product called Rid-X. It's intended to be used in septic tanks to increase the microbial action. The stuff is a powder and is super safe in your holding tanks. Buy it at hardware stores and plumbing shops in rural areas. Some Walmart stores carry it in the plumbing department. Use a couple of tablespoons after each time you dump the tanks.

7. GET IT ON THE LEVEL

An RV refrigerator repairman told me that a refrigerator could be ruined in an hour of running if it were not level. That sounds a little extreme but he may be right. Since replacing a fridge can cost enough to buy fuel for 8,000 miles of RVing, we shouldn't take chances. That means when we stop for lunch we should either park fairly level or turn the refrigerator off. It takes only a couple of minutes to do it. (Actually, you should leave the refrigerator off when you're traveling. Unless the weather is extremely hot, the refrigerator temperature won't rise enough to cause trouble.) Also, we should take the time when parking overnight to get level. It's easy if you have a couple of items of equipment.

You need a level, of course, but not just any old level will do. The instructions with your refrigerator say to place a bubble level on one of the ice cube racks in the freezing compartment and level both lengthwise and crosswise. The trouble is that you can't see the bubble when the level is on that rack. I think I have a better way. Buy one of those large levels made to fasten to the front of your trailer. Don't get one of the little dinky ones. Mount it on the front of the trailer where you can see it from the driver's seat. I use a small level placed on the bottom of the refrigerator and level the trailer both ways. Then adjust that big level on the front of the trailer so that it agrees, both ways.

Then make yourself a set of leveling blocks. Cut pieces of 2 X 6 lumber 60 inches, 54 inches, 48 inches, and 42 inches long. Cut one end at an angle. Back your trailer into position. Read the front level. Mine is marked so that each division on the level is about an inch off level. Then pull forward a short distance. Place the needed number of pieces of the leveling block in a stack behind the low wheels. Back up slowly until you see the bubble in the middle. Block the trailer wheels so they won't roll. Unhitch and level front to rear using the hitch jack. Nothing to it. Takes me about 2 minutes. Well, maybe 5.

8. THIS RIG SHOULDN'T BE ROCKING

Spending even a few hours in an RV that jiggles and rocks every time someone moves is no fun. Get at least a pair of adjustable stabilizer stands. Long trailers will need four. With the trailer level, set a stand under each rear corner and adjust the height to just touch the underside of the frame. Be sure to use the heavy, lengthwise frame members. Then give each jack screw one more turn. Do the same with a pair near the front if you want to. Makes things nice and solid.

Motorhomers who don't have an expensive automatic leveling system should have two small levels. After setting the rig level as mentioned above for trailers, mount one small level on the dash where you can see it while driving. Mount the other one to the wall on your left where you can see it. Then you won't have to climb out of the driver's seat to know if you're on the level. You will also know about how many blocks need to go under which wheels to finish the job.

9. GOTTA HAVE PRESSURE

Tire pressure, that is, and it had better be right. Unless tires have adequate pressure for the load, your tires will flex too much. This causes heat which results in early death for tires. Find out how much weight you're working with and how much air pressure you need to carry that weight safely. Get yourself a good tire gauge and use it frequently. If your tires can take the pressure, an extra five pounds over minimum carrying pressure won't hurt. Your tire dealer will have inflation charts that will help you determine the right pressure for you.

10. LEAKY ROOFS

RV manufacturers brag about their use of one-piece aluminum roofs. And rightly so. Those of us who have been around RVs for a while know what it was like before. But one-piece roofs have lots of holes in them, too. Holes for such things as ventilators, the vent for the holding tank, refrigerators, air conditioners. These are all potential leaks. Roof leaks unattended sooner or later become big problems with rotten frames, matted insulation, and ruined ceilings.

Fix that leak now! Get some aluminum roof cement from your hardware store or RV dealer. It's a sticky, black material. After cleaning all loose debris from around those things that stick through your roof, coat the areas with the cement. Then cover the cement with aluminum roof coating. This is a shiny material and is very important. Without it, the heat will shrink the black cement and you'll still have the leaks. Your dealer won't tell you, but you should put a coating of the silvery material around all of those roof projections every year.

11. BALANCE YOUR BRAKES

Trailer brakes that don't properly synchronize with the tow vehicle are a nuisance and can be a serious hazard. All brake controllers have an adjustment to set the amount of trailer braking. Too much and every stop is a jerk and wears trailer tires faster than necessary. Not enough and the tow vehicle is doing too much work and you don't have as much braking power as you need. You can get it right by working with the adjustment. When you come to a stop the trailer brakes should be very slightly noticeable as they apply. That keeps things where they belong with the trailer behind the tow vehicle.

With some trailer/tow vehicle combinations, there isn't enough adjustment to eliminate the heavy jerking from the trailer. Your dealer has an adjustable resistance pad that mounts in the electrical brake line between the controller and the trailer. Get one and make your stops more comfortable.

13. GETTING A CHARGE OUT OF IT

A constant challenge to trailer owners is keeping the battery charged. The problem is that very rarely does anyone put in a charging wire large enough to carry the current. Part of the difficulty is that the Bargman plug used to connect electric circuits between tow vehicle and trailer will not take a wire of adequate size.

Most people will tell you a #8 wire will do the job. It hasn't worked for me. I finally went to a welding supply dealer and bought enough #6 flexible copper wire to run two wires from the engine compartment to the trailer battery. One is hooked to the hot side of the starter solenoid and runs to the positive side of the trailer battery. The other runs from the negative side to a GOOD ground near the engine.

Obviously, a big disconnect plug is necessary. I got one from an industrial truck dealer. It comes in two identical matching parts. Each part is 2 inches by one and one-half inch. Make sure that you connect them so that positive goes to positive and negative to negative. Mount one beside your Bargman plug on the hitch platform. The whole thing cost less than $30, wire and plugs, and for the first time in 25 years I have a charging circuit that works.

13. NASTY WATER

Sooner or later you're going to get something in your water tank that shouldn't be there. Most likely it will be some sort of bacteria in the air or maybe a bad load of water. It makes little difference where it originated. You want to get rid of it. Household bleach is the best stuff. Use one-quarter cup of bleach for each 15 gallons of tank capacity. Mix the bleach into a gallon of water and pour it into the water tank. Fill the water tank. Open each faucet for 30 seconds to make sure the bleach gets through the lines. Let set for three hours. Drain completely and flush with clean water. Flush and drain again. That will sanitize the tank. Any residual chlorine will only be a nuisance. If it is too much nuisance, add a quart of vinegar for each five gallons of water and let set for a day. Drain and refill. That should do it.

14. VARMINTS

If you've ever opened your RV after a family of mice has spent the winter in your pride and joy, you won't want it to happen again. Why is it that RV manufacturers spend so much time and money installing insulation and then leave holes large enough for mice? Admittedly, a mouse doesn't require a very large opening, but I don't think they should be able to find any. Anyway, you've got them and don't want them. The answer? Close ALL openings.

From your friendly hardware dealer, buy a spray can of foam. Crawl under and spray the stuff in all openings regardless of how small they seem to be. Make sure you get them closed. Then from inside the RV, look into all floor-level storage areas. Spray the foam in all openings. Then you have only the problem of getting rid of any unwanted wildlife that may still be in your RV. A hungry cat, big dog, a stick of dynamite, or a bit of poison carefully used should suffice.

15. WHAT'S THIS BIG HOSE FOR, DAD?

That's the sewer hose, Son, and it is to be used EVERY TIME you empty the holding tank. There are lots of RVers who seem to think that it is okay just to pull up to the dumping station apron and open the valves. Not so. One result of the mess they leave is that many dumping stations have been closed. Use your hose. Keep an old pair of gloves handy if you don't want to get your hands dirty.

The procedure is simple. Hook up the sewer hose to your outlet. Insert the other end into the dumping station. Open the black water valve and let it drain first. Then open the gray water valve. That way you flush all the black water and solids out of your sewer hose. Put the sewer hose back in its container. Use the water hose that should be there to clean up. Close the dumping station. No problem.

Some RVers leave the valves open when they are in a park that has full hook-ups. Not a good idea. The solids tend to settle out instead of flowing through the line. There just isn't enough liquid. It's better to keep the valves closed until the tank is about half full and then open them. That way there's enough liquid to clean out the solids and your holding tank solution has time to break down some of the solids.

16. CHECKLIST

Ever had the refrigerator door come open while you're merrily tooling down the road and dump a dozen eggs and a bottle of beer on the carpet? That shouldn't happen and wouldn't happen if you had a checklist. Pilots always use one to make sure everything is operating as it should. You should, too. Make your own. Include all the things that need to be done before moving your RV, things like locking the refrigerator door and turning off the water pump. Then use the list. You'll save yourself lots of grief.

17. CLOSET ROD

No, not the one you hang your clothes on. I'm talking about the one that keeps the hangers on the rod. We very quickly got tired of having half the hangers fall every time we moved our RV. So, I went to the hardware store and bought an adjustable spring rod normally used to hold a curtain. When we're ready to move, we just slip it against the top of the closet rod. Spring tension holds it in place and the hangers can't jump off. Make sure the top buttons are buttoned on all garments so they won't fall off their hangers. Result, no messed up clothes and dirtied up attitude.

18. BOOKS AND MAGAZINES

Face it, we all like to take along some reading material. RVs are small living quarters so things left lying around make a real mess. Even if you're not a good carpenter, you can build a small plywood magazine rack with one-inch pine sides. Or, make a small book shelf out of similar materials. Stain to match your paneling and hang in one of those spaces not used by cabinets. Use toggle bolts to attach the units to the paneling.

You'll be glad you did.

19. POWER LINE ADAPTERS

Most of us plug into a park power line at least occasionally. It would be nice if all parks used the same kind of plugs, but they don't. Not being able to hook up when you want to can be very irritating. Solve the problem by buying a couple of adapters from your RV dealer before you leave home. They don't cost much.

20. POLAR PROBLEMS

While you're buying the adapters, also buy a gadget to check the polarity and ground of the park electrical outlets. Some parks have been wired by people who either didn't know the difference or were just careless. The result for you can be a shocking experience. Your life is worth more than the $10 the gadget costs.

21. HAPPINESS IS HAVING YOUR OWN HOSE

Have you ever wondered whether the hose you use to fill your water tank might have been in some dirty joints? Unless you're using your own hose, you can be sure it has. Some folks just don't care about their health. They use the drinking water hose to rinse out their holding tank and sewer hose and drive on. Buy a good 50-foot, five-eighths-inch diameter hose and know the company it keeps.

Also buy a water thief. It's a doo-hickey that attaches to one end of your water hose and slips over the occasional water faucet that does not have hose threads. Very convenient when you need it.

22. GET REALLY ORGANIZED

Let's see now. You carry that 50-foot hose and a heavy-duty electrical cord and stuff them into one of your outside storage compartments. What a rat's nest! Make a couple of reels out of scraps of plywood. Or you can buy a hose and reel combination from your friendly RV dealer. The hose and cord will last longer, and you will avoid tangles and temper tantrums.

23. THAT RUNNING-ON-EMPTY FEELING

Sooner or later, you're going to run out of water before you run out of time. You could always move the rig to a water outlet and fill the tank again, but it hardly seems worth the trouble. Carry along a plastic water tote for those short refills. There are at least two kinds. One is a collapsible bag that holds about 4 gallons. When it's empty, it takes up almost no space. The only problem is that it's tough to pour water from it. No shape. The other type looks like a GI can and holds 5 gallons. Worth its weight in gold -- well, feathers -- when you need just a few more gallons of water.

24. WATER, WATER EVERYWHERE...

A fact of modern life is that more and more of our drinking water contains things that we would rather not think about. There is probably no filter that will get out all possible pollutants, but buy the best you can find. You want more than just a filter. Purifiers do a better job.

25. SWEEP IT OUT

If vertical storage space is a bit short in your rig, too short to hold a full size broom, get a short broom. Buy a child's broom. Better yet, buy a full-size broom and cut the handle to fit your storage space.

26. PIPE CARRIER

Not your smoke pipe, Bunky. There always seems be long, skinny things like fishing rods or grill tripods that clutter up the place. They are also in danger of getting broken or tripping the dog. Make a storage tube out of a piece of plastic sewer pipe. Fit screw-in plugs at both ends. Fasten in front of the rear bumper or across the frame just in front of the trailer body. Pipe strap makes it easy.

27. LOID

That's the term for using a piece of plastic like a credit card to open a locked door. Avoid unwelcome house guests by installing a deadbolt lock. If your RV came with a deadbolt you're still not safe. Most RV locks are designed to be opened with a master key. That makes it easy for dealers to open several RV doors every morning without having to carry a ton of keys. Getting your locks re-keyed is a simple job for any locksmith.

28. A STEP AT A TIME

By the time you get your RV parked and leveled, you will often find that the first step up or down is a big one. Make it easy on yourself with a landing platform built from scraps of plywood. No scraps? You'll have them after you've built the other things I mentioned. The platform should be large enough that it won't tip over easily when you step on it. About 18 inches square by 6 inches high will work well.

29. GALLEY ORGANIZERS

I'm not talking about labor unions here. I'm talking about that mess in the galley storage compartments. Every time you move the rig, all those boxes and cans and jars seem to take on a life of their own. Your RV dealer and the local variety store have lots of plastic organizers to hold things in their places. You'll need a variety of them.

30. COVER UP

The next time you have to change a tire or crawl under the rig or do a dirty repair job, you'll wish you had some "dirty job" clothes. Carry a pair of old coveralls or an old shirt and jeans and put them on at the first sign of trouble.

31. KNEELING BOARD

Every time you hitch up, you'll be glad you brought along a piece of plywood to kneel on. A piece 24 inches square will save a lot of dirty knees and help preserve domestic tranquillity.

32. HITCH LOCK

Coming back from seeing a beautiful glacier only to find your trailer has wandered off can ruin your day. Have you ever thought how easy it would be for someone with a trailer hitch to back up to yours while you're out seeing the sights? Nightmares! Avoid the possibility by locking the hitch. Some latches have a hole to accept a padlock. If you can't open the latch, it's tough to hitch up. But not impossible. Better yet is to lock a spare ball in the hitch. Better still is to buy a special lock for the ball socket. Peace of mind is easily worth the few bucks one costs.

33. DON'T SIGN HERE

RV folks are just naturally friendly. Some of us are so friendly that we like for everybody to know who we are. So, we hang out a cute little sign "Jack and Mary Smith of Cleveland." It may be friendly but it is definitely not a good idea. If I walked up to your rig in the middle of the night, knocked on the door and said "Hey, Jack, give me hand here" the odds are that you would open the door. While I wouldn't hurt you -- I'm just a friendly RVer -- the next guy who calls you by name might not be so friendly.

34. IN THE SHADE

When the sun us bright and the air is hot, most of us like to sit in the shade. Your tires do, too. In fact, they like the shade any time they aren't moving. Too much sun can age our skin quickly, and too much sunlight can age your tires quickly. The flexing of the tires as they move down the road releases compounds that counteract the deteriorating effects of sunlight. But when your RV sits and the tires get no action, the sunlight gets in its bad licks. Protect your tires by putting them in the shade. Make covers out of fabric or cut some pieces of that handy dandy plywood to lean against the tires. Your wallet will feel the difference.

35. PLEASE SQUEEZE

We've all had the experience of arriving at the old campground to find 40 miles of paper towel and toilet tissue on the floor. Put the squeeze on the paper roll enough to mash it so that the center loses its round shape and the roll won't unroll when you don't want it to. Simple.

36. LINE YOUR NEST

Space is usually at premium in our RVs. So it is only natural that we nest small pans inside large pans. The problem is that if those pans are lined with Teflon or Silverstone, the lining gets scratched. Protect your pans with some sort of soft material. Place a dishrag between them. They'll love you for it.

37. DON'T GROW YOUR OWN

You've come back to your RV after a week of inactivity and found that greenish gray gunk growing on the shelves and walls of your refrigerator? It makes no difference that you cleaned well before you closed up. That stuff just loves to grow in warm, dark places. Leave the fridge door open while the power is off and the stuff won't grow. Now, of course, if you like greenish gray gunk....

38. BOX IT

Underseat storage is good to have, but it does have one shortcoming. Anything placed there tends to melt together as your RV does its thing down the road. Find some boxes the right size to fit the space and keep things separate. Maybe a box for each person or type of material. Those boxes in which offices get their paper seem to fit most underseat spaces well. Liquor boxes are good, too.

39. ISOLATION BOOTH

At least twice we've arrived in camp to find our RV smelling like a brewery and an upper storage area dripping. Not good. It seems that aluminum drink cans are very thin and tend to develop holes when they rub together. The resulting pressurized leak is a mess. One way to solve it is to buy your soft drinks in bottles and store them so that they can't fall over. But if you like cans, then find a way to make sure they can't rub shoulders. If you find a surefire way, let me know. I'm not happy with anything we've tried.

40. COOL IT

Your dealer probably told you that your motorhome or tow vehicle with an automatic transmission has a built-in transmission cooler and doesn't need anything more. Wrong. Very wrong. As in "expensive." If you put a temperature gauge on your tranny, you'll get scared and smart very quickly. I urge you to put on such a gauge. And I urge you to install an auxiliary transmission cooler. Even several minutes of operation with the transmission fluid at a temperature above 250 degrees -- not uncommon while climbing hills on a hot day -- can significantly lower its lubricating qualities. That means an early death to the tranny and an expensive repair bill. Spend your money on an auxiliary transmission cooler of ample size.

41. YOUR ENGINE'S GOTTA TURN

But not too much and not too slow. Buying a tow vehicle with the proper gearing these days can be a problem. That's especially true if you buy a used one. Most vehicles come from the factory with such high gearing (low numerical) that they don't tow very well. If that's your problem, you may have considered having the gears in the differential changed to higher numbers. That's fine for towing but not so good when unhooked. For about twice the price of new differential gears you can have the best for both situations. Buy an under-drive unit. Then you've got the good solo gearing your vehicle came with and good towing gears when you need them. The same thing works for motorhomes that don't have quite enough muscle for the mountains. If your tow vehicle has lower gearing than you need when running solo, you might want to consider an overdrive.

42. FLAPS DOWN

Tired of washing the mud and scrubbing the road oil off the front of your trailer? Do you wish you could avoid chipping paint from your LP-gas bottles and your trailer's A-frame? You can. Put heavy mudflaps on the rear of your tow vehicle. The best are the large ones that extend all the way across. Another type looks like a big moustache hanging from the back bumper of the tow vehicle or motorhome. It works great.

43. SHIFT YOUR GEARS

Too many RVers with an automatic transmission feel that the box knows best when to shift. Not so. When climbing hills, you can easily lug the engine down too far before the transmission shifts. The result is that your engine is running too slowly to develop the power needed, engine and transmission temperatures rise, and the fuel level drops faster than necessary. Don't be afraid to shift the gears manually. If road speed decreases 10 mph, it's time to shift to a lower gear. That's just a rule of thumb. Better is to use a tachometer and keep engine speed near the engine's best torque speed. Or use a vacuum gauge and shift when vacuum falls below six or seven inches.

44. SILICONE TREATMENT

As much as we try to avoid them, puncture wounds do occur. If they occur to your RV's skin, one of the best repairs is a small squirt of clear silicone. The stuff is also good to seal intentional punctures such as when you mount something to the RV skin. You can buy it at any hardware store.

45. SCREW IT

There are lots of screws in any RV and some come loose. Walk around your RV and note the different kinds and sizes. Then go to your hardware store and buy a few of each type and size and keep them in the rig. Be sure to buy either stainless steel or aluminum. Even cadmium coated screws will rust eventually and make nasty stains. Also buy any special type screw drivers needed. Periodically inspect your rig and tighten/replace loose fasteners. If the same fastener keeps coming loose, try putting a dab of that silicone sealer on the threads and snug it down.

46. DEEP-CYCLE IT

Some new RVers try to use a regular automobile battery as the auxiliary battery in their RV. They don't work well. The problem is that the aux battery gets discharged much more deeply between charges than does the battery that starts the engine. Auto batteries aren't designed for that kind of service and mug themselves if made to discharge deeply. Service life for an auto battery in RV use is likely to be less than two years. Get a deep-cycle battery such as used in marine use. Most of them are now marked RV/marine use. They are designed for deep discharge and will usually last about five years. There are now some maintenance-free deep-cycle batteries that never require additional water. Worth checking into.

47. REMOVE THE CAPS

I know that hubcaps on your trailer wheels look nice. But lug bolts do work loose. Good operating procedure is to check all lug bolts at least once a week when on the road. If the hubcaps are in place, you won't do it. Take them off. Haven't bought any yet? Don't.

48. PACK IT IN

RV wheel bearings take a beating. They sit for long periods of time and then suddenly have to carry a heavy load at high speeds on hot days. The bearing grease needs to be cleaned out and replaced every couple of years or 15,000 miles, whichever comes first. It isn't a tough job, but it can be messy. If you're not sure how to do it, you can learn by reading back issues of "Trailer Life" or checking any good car or truck repair manual. If you don't want to do it yourself, get your RV dealer to do it. But do it.

49. EQUIP IT

Some folks try to economize by hauling things such as pots and pans, other kitchenware, and linens back and forth from house to RV. Those folks soon tire of the extra aggravation and don't use their RVs as much as they would like. Treat your RV to its own set of equipment. If you want to keep the cost to a minimum, buy at rummage sales. Most longtime RVers will even have jackets and other clothes that are kept in the RV. If your RV is ready to go at five minutes' notice, you'll use it more and have more fun.

50. DRIVE IT

I'll admit that this is a pet peeve. Nearly every weekend trip, I find myself behind an RV going 45 mph when there is no traffic or road condition demanding that low a speed. Traffic lines up behind the RV, and soon drivers become angry and take dangerous chances. There is rarely a reason for driving less than 55. If you must drive slower than the rest of traffic find a spot to pull off and let them pass as soon as possible. It's only courteous to do so. Driving 50 instead of 55 will save you less than 1 mile per gallon but it will make lots of enemies for us all.

Chapter 2

Air Conditioners And Attic Fans

The temperature outside this morning was 12 degrees. Snow fell last night, and my first job after breakfast was to shovel the drive. The next is to write about air conditioners and fans.

It's a funny business. But by the time you read this, some of you will be sweltering in South Texas, Arizona, Florida, or some equally hot part of the country. And even Wisconsin gets hot enough to make some form of cooling assistance welcome sooner than seems possible.

RVing has become such a popular activity, with RVers roaming from Canada to Mexico in all of the weather extremes imaginable, that auxiliary cooling has become almost as necessary as a furnace. Nearly all Class A motorhomes and some Class C's now come with cab air conditioning as standard equipment. While fewer travel trailers come from the factory with air conditioning, rare is the trailer that is not pre-wired and ready for easy installation. Finding a large RV of any type without air conditioning would be difficult in the southern states during the summer.

And with good reason. Air conditioners have dropped in price to the extent that they are no longer the most expensive RV accessory. Installation is so easy that many owners do it themselves. With electricity available in many public and all private campgrounds, power is seldom a problem.

THREE SIZES FIT ALL

Air conditioners are available in three sizes to fit the needs of all RVers. Ratings are in British Thermal Units (BTU), with most manufacturers offering units rated for 7,100, 11,000, and 13,500 BTU. One BTU is the amount of energy needed to raise the temperature of a pound of water one degree Fahrenheit. What's that you say? You're interested in cooling, not heating? I agree, but an air conditioner works by using the heat in the air inside your RV to raise the temperature of the air outside the RV. An air conditioner is simply a heat transfer device. An easy way to rate its power is to consider how well it transfers that heat from inside to outside.

Trying to find a rule for how much air conditioning capacity or power is needed for a given size RV is about like trying to find a solution to the national debt. I talked with manufacturers' representatives and with RV dealers. The result was always, "Well,it depends." And it does.

To take one extreme, I have used a trailer for nearly 30 years, but not one has had an air conditioner. That's because I don't like hot weather and avoid it when possible. I'm from Wisconsin, where it can get hot enough to melt a bill collector's heart, but the hot weather seldom lasts very long. I've used a trailer in nearly every state but selected my times to avoid the worst of the hot weather. But I can see the time not too far in the future when an air conditioner will be welcome. I would like to spend some extended periods in the desert regions of the Southwest. It gets hot there.

So, one factor in selecting an air conditioner is where and when you expect to be using the RV. Another factor is the amount of insulation in the RV. Insulation helps to keep the warm air inside in the winter and outside in the summer. Many RVs are insulated to an R-value of 5. Others have a value of 7 or 9 and the roofs of some quality RVs are insulated to a value of 12 or higher. The more insulation, the less the cooling load.

SIZE OF RV IS MOST IMPORTANT

Even the color of the roof can be important. Dark roofs absorb much more heat from the sun than white or aluminum colored roofs. A roof that has been recently coated with aluminum sealer will absorb less heat than an older, dirty roof.

And, of course, the size of the RV is important in deciding the amount of cooling capacity needed. One RV dealer who has been in the business for many years finally admitted to me that when all of those factors were considered, size was the important one. If the RVer feels he or she needs an air conditioner, this dealer would install one 11,000-BTU unit if the RV were under 22 feet or one 13,500-BTU unit if the RV were between 22 and 30 feet. Larger RVs would get two 13,500-BTU units.

Air conditioners can also be used as heaters. Most air conditioners can have an optional 5,600-BTU electric heating strip installed. These would likely be most attractive to Snowbirds and others who spend a lot of time in moderately cool weather in resort parks. For serious heating, the furnace would be needed.

Prices of air conditioners, of course, vary. Camping World, a large chain of RV accessory stores, lists prices from $549 for a 7,100-BTU to a 13,500-BTU at $749. Local dealers would probably charge a bit more. Having a local installer to talk with if things go wrong can be an advantage.

DO-IT-YOURSELF INSTALLATION

Installation of most units is easy in RVs manufactured within the past five years. Nearly all RVs are now built with roof reinforcement and wiring for an air conditioner. If that is the case with yours and you are reasonably handy with tools, you can probably install the unit yourself. If you don't want to try it, most dealers charge only about $50 for installation. The $50 looks like a bargain. Weights of most units run around 75 to 90 pounds, and dropping one while carrying it to the top of your RV would be more expensive than a dealer's installation cost. Let him drop it. Too, it's nice to have someone to yell at if a problem develops.

Depending upon where you travel, you might not need an air conditioner. There are two other devices that may be adequate and cost considerably less. Evaporative coolers were popular in homes in the Southwest 50 years ago. Some people still use them. The principle of operation is at once simple and mysterious. Air is blown through a filter that is kept constantly moist. As the air passes through the moist filter, some of the water from the filter is evaporated. The evaporation process demands heat, which is taken from the air. The result is cooled air.

Obviously, the process works best in regions that have a low humidity. In those parts of the country, mainly the Southwestern states, the system works quite well. For example, if the outside air is at 95 degrees with a relative humidity of 25%, the temperature of air passing through an evaporative cooler will be lowered to about 82 degrees.

Evaporative coolers for RVs are available from Camping World or Recair, 26690 Wagonwheel Drive, Pioneer, CA 95666. Two advantages of evaporative coolers have to do with cost. They sell for about half the price of an air conditioner. But the savings don't stop there. Most can be powered by either your 12-volt battery or 110 volts. Power demand on 12 volts runs from 3.2 amps to 7.2 amps, depending on size of the unit and fan speed. The larger figure is enough to make you take care not to run the battery down, but the lower figure is relatively insignificant.

The water for cooling operation is contained in a tray that is part of the unit. The tray can be refilled by hand or hooked up to the RV's water system. Some units can be attached to a garden hose for automatic operation. On some units, the fan can be reversed to act as an exhaust fan, pulling the hot air out of the RV. Installation of an evaporative cooler is so easy that nearly any RV owner can do it.

EXHAUST FANS

Exhaust fans are the third and least expensive method of cooling an RV. All of us are familiar with the exhaust fan built into the ventilator in RV bathrooms. Larger fans can also be installed to replace the ventilators for more effective use. These fans act just like the attic fans that are popular in homes in warmer parts of the country. The principle of operation is twofold. Removing the hot air from inside the RV draws in outside air which may be cooler. A difference of even a few degrees can add to the comfort.

A larger cooling benefit comes from the evaporative effect when air moves over our bodies. Our bodies perspire when we are warm. The surrounding air absorbs the perspiration and slightly cools our skin. The principle is the same as the evaporative cooler mentioned earlier.

Moving air from a breeze increases the effect. In the winter, we refer to the additional cooling effect of moving air as the wind chill factor. I was very aware of it this morning while shoveling snow.

If an exhaust fan is used and windows are opened so as to direct the moving air across our bodies, the result can be greatly increased comfort. An important point to remember is that the air does not have to be moving very fast to obtain optimum results. About three mph is best. A higher air speed can soon become uncomfortably cool.

The best arrangement with an exhaust fan is to open only the windows that will allow air to pass over our bodies. Leaving the other windows closed increases the speed of the air that does enter and increases the cooling effect.

Exhaust fans cost from $170 to nearly $400. Kool-O-Matic, P.O. Box 310, Niles, MI 49120, has several different sizes. Some can be equipped with a remote thermostat similar to the one on your furnace. If the air temperature drops to a preset level during the night, the fan will turn off. Most exhaust fans run off the 12-volt system in your RV. Some of the larger ones operate on 110 volts. There is at least one model that is solar powered with its own panel for collecting energy from the sun.

Exhaust fans replace the standard ventilators in RVs. Installation is very easy. For both evaporative coolers and exhaust fans, installation consists of removing an existing ventilator, applying sealer on exterior surfaces, dropping the unit into place and tightening everything down. Units that operate on 110 volts can be plugged into the existing air conditioner pre-wiring.

KEEP IT CLEAN

Maintenance of fans and air conditioners consists mainly of keeping things clean. Filters must be changed or cleaned periodically. Debris such as leaves and twigs should be removed. Condenser and evaporator coils on air conditioners should be vacuumed occasionally to keep dust and dirt from accumulating. Most units require no lubrication, but check your owner's manual to be sure.

Easy. Even I can do it.

No longer do we have to just put up with the weather. We can at least modify the climate inside our RVs with one of the cooling units discussed here. And of course, if the weather is too uncomfortable, we can always move to a better climate. That's one of the advantages of having an RV.

Now if I can just dig our trailer out of that snowbank. Where did I put that shovel?

Chapter 3

Batteries: Try Going Maintenance-Free

Tired of wondering whether your RV accessory battery -- the one that powers all those lights and other goodies while you're parked -- needs water or the terminals are corroded and the charge isn't getting through?

Me, too.

I do know that with the frequent, heavy charges necessary to keep my RV battery ready and able to supply my needs, the water does seem to get away. I also know that if I don't check and refill it frequently, it will soon go belly-up.

Well, Ol' Buddy, there's a relatively new battery on the market that is sealed so that not only don't you have to worry about the water level, but you couldn't add any if you tried. It doesn't emit the usual gases and vapors so it doesn't get corroded terminals. And it will give you up to 30% longer life. Not too shabby.

Maintenance-free batteries for normal vehicle use -- starting, ignition, lights -- have been around for several years, but they haven't worked in deep-cycle service, the kind of use we give them in RVs. Now there are at least three new sealed, maintenance-free batteries on the market for deep-cycle service. And they work.

HOW THEY OPERATE

In order to understand the new battery technology, we need to take a look at what happens in lead-acid storage batteries, the kind we use in our RVs and other vehicles. First, we have to understand that lead-acid batteries don't generate electricity; they act only as storage units. Each cell in a battery consists of lead alloy plates separated by insulating material with the whole thing immersed in a solution of sulfuric acid. In conventional batteries, the lead is alloyed with antimony. If we connect a charged battery to a load such as a light or water pump, oxygen in the form of lead peroxide migrates from the positive plate to the negative plate, releasing electricity into the circuit. The process continues as long as there is an excess of lead peroxide on the positive plate. As the process continues, the voltage drops until the battery is discharged.

If the battery is connected to a circuit with a higher than cell voltage, as with a charger or your vehicle alternator, the process is reversed. Electrons move back through the cell, reversing the chemical action and restoring the plates to their original condition. Continued charging current then causes the water in the acid solution to split by electrolysis into oxygen and hydrogen. Oxygen collects at the positive plate and hydrogen collects at the negative. Being gases, both are released to the atmosphere through the vents in the battery case. This can occur even in a properly adjusted system and accounts for the loss of water in conventional batteries. It also accounts for the potentially explosive condition that surrounds a charging battery and is why batteries should always be kept in well-ventilated areas. (Am I the only one who worries about the potential for disaster with the way batteries are contained in some RVs?)

LESS WATER IS LOST

In maintenance-free batteries, calcium-lead alloy is used instead of the antimony-lead found in conventional batteries. Less water is lost, but some does escape. In normal vehicle use, the battery is seldom more than slightly discharged. The charging process usually lasts only

several minutes, and the loss of water is so slight as to be of no consideration. Deep-cycle batteries, however, are usually heavily discharged from using RV lights and accessories over a weekend or longer, or from similar heavy use. The subsequent charging process may take hours. Loss of water becomes important.

Manufacturers of the new maintenance-free deep cycle batteries claim to have changed all this by using an oxygen-recombination process. Instead of the plates being immersed in a liquid sulfuric acid solution, they are sandwiched between layers of felt-like glass fiber which are partially saturated with the acid solution. This forces the oxygen to move across the cell rather than escaping. The negative plate is larger than normal and made of highly reactive lead to absorb this free oxygen as oxides. As the charging current continues, the oxygen is released back into the solution instead of escaping. The effect is that the negative plate never reaches a fully charged state. No hydrogen is produced. No oxygen escapes. No additional water is needed.

Since no gases can escape and no water ever needs to be added, the battery case can be sealed. There are pressure vents to act as safety measures in the event that a seriously malfunctioning charge system should ever be used. But normal service, even the kind of severe use encountered in RVs, never permits the kind of pressures that would activate the vents.

NO TERMINAL CORROSION

One benefit, in addition to not needing water is that there is no corrosion to terminals. Terminal corrosion is caused by a chemical reaction between the escaping hydrogen and the lead terminal posts. Some vehicle manufacturers have tried to avoid terminal corrosion by placing the terminals out of the area of escaping hydrogen on the sides of the cases. This new design eliminates the problem entirely. One caution. Even though normal use does not generate escaping hydrogen, there is always the possibility that a malfunction in the charging circuit could permit a serious overcharge condition. These batteries should still be located in a ventilated environment.

Charging does call for a particular approach. The charging current must be tapering. That is, the current must taper to near zero as the battery approaches full charge. That is the way a normally operating vehicle charge system functions. Most small battery chargers also function this way. Some do not. Check yours and see if the ammeter moves lower as the battery reaches full charge. Also, do not use the maintenance-free setting on your charger if it is so equipped.

The manufacturers claim the following advantages for their new batteries:

1. Use of the new design separators allows up to 30% more deep cycles than standard deep cycle batteries.

2. No acid fumes. No spillage. No corrosion.

3. Since the battery case is sealed, there is no danger from an overturned battery. Batteries should still be firmly mounted to avoid movement.

4. Never any maintenance needed.

5. Compact design permits the same power as a conventional deep cycle battery but in a smaller package. In actual practice, the batteries from the three companies I was able to check are the same size as conventional deep cycle batteries of the same capacity.

THE PRICE TO PAY

Now the down side. There is always a price to pay for significant improvements. Milwaukee prices quoted to me were $80-$90 for the Delco Voyager, $80 for the GNB Stowaway, $70 for the Pacific Chloride Torque Starter, and about $50 for the conventional GNB Action Pack. Costs, then, are from 40% to 80% higher than for the popular Action Pack. Against this, claims are for 30% more cycles. And don't forget the significant benefits of total freedom from maintenance and the safety of no escaping hydrogen. These extra benefits cost from $5 to $25, which isn't a lot when spread over the lifetime of your battery, 3 to 5 years.

For additional information contact: Delco Remy Division, General Motors Corporation, P.O. Box 2439, Anderson, IN 46018-9986.

GNB Incorporated, Automotive Battery Division, P.O. Box 64100, St. Paul, MN 55164-0100.

Pacific Chloride, Inc., P.O. Box 1124, Tampa, FL 33601.

Chapter 4

Bike Racks: Take Two For Fun

One of the best additions ever to my camping/traveling gear was a motorcycle. Now, don't get all bent out of shape. It's not a big, noisy beast, but it will handle two full-size adults easily. And no one has yet claimed it's a nuisance in any campground. I carry it easily on our RV and so could you.

Even if you now tow a car behind your motorhome for sightseeing trips and errands, you will find a dozen uses every day for a small motorcycle or scooter.

Let me tell you about some of the ways I use my "bike," and you may decide you don't even need to drag that car behind you. For openers, let's take a look at how I carry mini. I have a simple rack that bolts to the rear frame of my trailer. The rack has an iron channel to hold the wheels. A set of supports made from perforated iron tubing serves to keep the bike in position without rubbing on the trailer.

I have another rack that clamps on the front bumper of my van for use when I don't want to carry the bike on the trailer. For this rack, I made a simple set of clamps from some polyethylene rope and two pieces of plastic pipe. These fasten the top of the bike to the van so that it doesn't rub. As to why I might want to carry the bike on the front of the van rather than the rear of the trailer, read on.

WEIGHT IS IMPORTANT

The bike weighs 215 pounds. Now that may sound like a lot, but I'll be 61 my next birthday, and I have no trouble getting it on the rack. I lift only one end at a time, and I can handle that much weight. If you can't lift that much, I'd suggest buying either a smaller bike or a scooter or one of the racks made with a ramp to roll the bike up.

My bike's 215 pounds includes full-size wheels for a comfortable ride and easy control, a seat big enough for two adults, and a 185 CC engine that will carry me at an easy 60 mph and give outstanding mileage. Most of my rides are at 25 to 45 mph while we travel side roads. At those speeds, I can expect to get 85 to 90 miles per gallon. At that rate, it doesn't take long for the bike to pay for itself in fuel saved. But there is no way to measure the fun. And there is no way to tell you how much more I see while riding the bike than when traveling the same roads in the RV. It's a different world.

Let's look at the ways RVers use small motorcycles as part of our camping gear.

When we are camping, we like to travel the back roads and fire trails, looking at the scenery. The bike is great for that. Without the structure of a car or van around us, we see a lot more. And if we want to go back to take a second look at something we just passed, the bike makes it easy.

We also use the bike for quick trips to the grocery store. A plastic "milk carton" type box strapped to the luggage rack can hold two large sacks of groceries. On our sightseeing trips, the same box holds camera equipment, a thermos or small cooler and extra jackets or sweaters.

Some campers carry a small motorcycle just for its "lifeboat" qualities. I met a family near Taos, New Mexico, that seldom uses their bike for anything else. If their tow vehicle breaks down, they have the bike to go for help. I have to admit that I have felt some comfort in knowing that the bike is available for those kinds of emergencies, too.

GOOD FOR BACKROADS TRAVEL

Lots of RVers find that an excellent fishing spot is eight or ten miles down a fire trail or jeep road -- farther than they want to walk and rougher than they want to drive the RV. A small motorcycle is perfect for their use. You don't need a trail bike; your small street bike will do. The same luggage rack that carries the grocery bags will carry a tackle box. A rod carrier can easily be made from a section of plastic pipe and strapped on the front or wherever convenient. The bike can go most places a pack mule can and doesn't mess up the campsite between trips.

There are some who think riding a motorcycle is acting out a death wish. While a motorcycle does offer less protection in an accident, there is nothing inherently dangerous about one. I have ridden bikes of various sizes for most of the last forty years, and I have yet to be scratched. I have always recognized that the bike can become boss the instant that I let it. But that is true of any type vehicle. I also practice safe driving habits.

For one thing, I never ride without my "brain bucket" -- a helmet approved by the Department of Transportation. Sure, having the wind blowing through my hair feels good. But having the assurance of no extra holes in my head feels better.

There are several choices in buying a helmet. Some people like a full-face type that covers the chin. I had one and found that for the kind of riding I do, it was more helmet than I wanted. I prefer the open-face type. Another choice is price. You can buy a DOT approved helmet at a discount store for under $35. You may find it comfortable. I had one of those that was all right for about fifteen minutes. After that it gave me a terrible headache from pressure spots over each eye. Maybe it was due to the shape of my block head! I finally spent the bucks and got myself a helmet I can wear all day. Find one that's comfortable.

OTHER SAFETY GEAR

I also always use either a visor attached to the helmet or a windscreen on the bike. Either will keep flying debris and bugs from hitting me in the eye. The windscreen is mounted to brackets on the handlebars and is easily detached for transporting by loosening four thumbscrews. Forget the notion that glasses will furnish you protection. A beetle or hornet or pebble at 45 mph will furnish your friendly ophthalmologist with an interesting couple of hours picking glass out of your eye. Do it right.

Other recommended safety equipment includes long pants and serviceable shoes. Shorts and sandals have no place on a motorcycle. If you have ever had a hornet find his way up a pair of shorts at 45 miles per hour, you will know what I mean. Flying gravel against bare toes is no picnic, either. You will likely find a long-sleeve shirt desirable, too. Without it, the built-in breeze keeps you cool enough that you won't notice the sunburn until it's too late.

Safety equipment also includes a careful mental attitude. The bike is not dangerous, but the driver may be. There are places where riding a bike at the legal speed limit is safe. There are other places where riding that fast may be possible but not safe. Loose gravel, wet leaves and rain puddles can be hazardous to your health. More care is needed with a bike than with several tons of RV around you.

Choosing a motorcycle or scooter to carry with you takes care. Weight of the bike becomes a factor. Someone -- you -- is going to have to load and unload it. There are racks that help you but you also have to consider the effect of the weight once it is loaded. An extra 200 pounds on the front of your RV likely won't make much difference, but an extra 300 pounds can overload tires or cause handling problems. I believe my 225-pound Yamaha is about the limit for portability.

At the same time, you want a bike that is large enough to be fairly comfortable and have enough power for the kind of riding you will do. Whether you will be riding solo or with a passenger is also a consideration. A passenger requires more power than riding solo. Some small bikes don't have the carrying capacity for a passenger. Even if you could install a larger seat, the tires and springs might be overloaded. Check the manufacturer's statement on capacity.

CONSIDER TIRE SIZE

Whether to get a small motorcycle or a motorscooter is another choice. Some prefer the style of one over the other. One important factor is the difference in tire diameter. Scooters have much smaller tires. Small diameter tires tend to be more affected by ruts and stones and other imperfections in the road surface. Large diameter tires more easily ride over the rough spots. I feel that the large tires of motorcycles are more easily controlled. Obviously, there are those who disagree.

Both scooters and bikes are available in sizes and with sufficient power for your needs. How much power is needed? Bikes and scooters are usually rated by engine size in cubic centimeters of displacement rather than by horsepower. I've tried small bikes from 85 CC to 185 CC. The 85 CC was marginal for two people. With one person, it easily ran about 45 mph. A passenger really made it slow down. A 125 CC handled two people adequately. The 185 CC I have now is great. Solo, it will run 65 mph with no problems. Two of us (I weigh 200) ride easily at 50.

A big problem in shopping for a small bike is the changing patterns of manufacturing. The factories prefer to build big bikes for big bucks. They may discontinue the small sizes for several years and then make a few for a couple of years. Often you can find a brand new bike that has been sitting in a dealer's back room for a couple of years just waiting for you.

Since you will want to ride on the road, you will need a bike that is street-legal. That means that it has such things as lights and a horn. There are a variety of so-called trail bikes that are not street-legal. Most of them are also quite noisy. Try to find a street bike. Most dealers will have a few new or used machines. Look around. You may luck out as I did and find a brand new bike that is just what you want that was left over from a couple of years back. That dealer still has an identical twin of mine. I got a good deal and so will another lucky buyer.

After you've made your selection, how do you carry it with you? There are several racks available. Some are good and some are marginal. I bought one that mounts to the bumpers of a car or truck. It has iron rings that fit around the wheels. But it has nothing to tie the bike to the truck. Although it is supposed to carry up to 250 pounds, that much weight really overloads the rack unless you build in additional supports as I did.

Most bikes are carried on the front of the RV or tow vehicle. If you tow a trailer, front mounting may be the only choice. With most trailers, adding the weight of a bike to the rear can aggravate a sway problem. The additional weight at the rear of the trailer makes the front end too light. I tried it with a Reese-type hitch and found the results unacceptable. Others have not had the problem.

If your trailer has an unusually heavy hitch weight, you might be able to get by with no problems. I now have a Pull-Rite hitch. Because of its unique design, I am able to carry my bike on the rear of the trailer with no problem.

Most bikes will need a better rack than the bumper-type mount whether the bike is carried on the front or the rear. Bumpers are just too springy even with additional support. Tote-N-Stow, 6301 Arthur, Merrillville, Indiana, makes a variety of racks that are sturdy and well designed. They have models either with a ramp to assist in loading the bike or with an electric lift if that is needed.

However you manage to take your bike or scooter with you, I know you will enjoy it. I use mine for several hundred miles of pleasant riding every summer. Whenever I go camping, there is no question of whether I take the bike. It goes.

Chapter 5

Brakes, and How To Care For Them

One of the scariest and most dangerous experiences in driving is to press on the brake pedal and have nothing happen. Many drivers will tell you that the vehicle actually speeded up. That's impossible, but it can certainly seem like it.

Good brakes are one of the most important systems on your RV or any other vehicle. Let's take a look at what needs to be done to ensure that when you push the stop pedal you will stop safely.

Since motorhomes and tow vehicles have many similarities in braking systems, we will start with them. When any vehicle is moving rapidly down the road, it has a terrific amount of energy stored in that motion. Physicists call it kinetic energy. The energy has the ability to keep the vehicle moving at high speed even after power from the engine is shut off.

If you simply stop supplying additional power from the engine, the vehicle will continue to roll until the kinetic energy is depleted in overcoming the rolling friction of the vehicle. That may take some time and a lot of space.

CREATING HEAT ENERGY

If, on the other hand, it is important that the vehicle be stopped quickly to avoid an accident or negotiate a traffic situation, the kinetic energy must be depleted some other way. You can't simply throw energy away; it has to be transformed into another form of energy or used to perform work. In the case of stopping a moving vehicle quickly, we transform the kinetic energy of motion into heat energy by applying the brakes.

When you push the pedal, brake shoes or pads at each wheel move out to bear against the corresponding brake drums or rotors. The shoes or pads are lined with high-friction materials. The harder you press the brake pedal, the harder the shoes or pads press against the drums or rotors. The friction materials produce a lot of heat and transform the kinetic energy to heat energy which is then used to warm the air surrounding the heated parts.

Some of the kinetic energy is also used to wear away the surfaces of the friction materials and corresponding brake parts. Eventually, the wear will be significant enough that the brakes are no longer efficient and must be repaired. That can happen in a very short time if the brakes are abused by frequently quick stops from high speed, or it can take many thousands of miles. But inevitably, brakes will need to be repaired.

There are other reasons for brake repairs. If you spend a lot of time driving in the northern states where your vehicle is exposed to road salt, rust can cause brake parts to stick. Dragging brakes or brakes that simply refuse to work can be the result. So can rusted steel brake lines that develop leaks. Foreign materials such as tiny bits of gravel or oil from leaking bearing seals can cause early repairs. Brakes on all modern vehicles have a power assist to reduce the needed pedal pressure. The assist comes from a vacuum or hydraulic booster. The booster can leak or fail and be another source for needed repairs.

It is safe to say that any time your brakes seem not to be operating correctly -- more than the normal amount of pressure is needed, unusual noises are produced, one or more wheels seem to be dragging, one or more wheels seem not to be producing any braking power -- it is time to ask your friendly mechanic to check your brakes.

GET REGULAR CHECK-UPS

It is even better to get regular check-ups. How often? Naturally, that depends. Large Class A motorhomes built on bus or custom-made chassis usually are built with so much extra strength that they need less frequent checking than do smaller motorhomes and tow vehicles.

Still, it pays to be safe. All tow vehicles, Class C motorhomes, and Class A's not built on bus chassis should have brake inspections at about 20,000 miles. If wear at that time is minimal and normal, check again in another 10,000 miles and each additional 10,000 miles until friction materials need to be replaced.

The largest Class A motorhomes probably ought to be checked at 50,000 miles and then each additional 15,000 miles until replacement. Obviously, towing a car will increase the wearing rate and decrease the time before replacement is needed.

Most Class C motorhomes and tow vehicles should have brake shoes or pads replaced when material is worn within an eighth inch of the rivets or metal parts. Repair brakes in pairs. If one front wheel needs repair, repair both wheels. Front wheels produce by far the greater part of the braking action and will need repairs more frequently than will rear wheels. I've found on my tow vehicles that front brakes will average around 70,000 miles before repairs are needed, with rear wheels giving around 110,000 miles.

The question always arises as to how extensive the repairs should be. Should the rotors and drums be turned? Do the wheel cylinders need to be rebuilt? And what are these parts?

Rotors and drums are the steel or cast iron parts attached to the rotating wheels of the vehicle. The friction materials bear against them and wear them down. The wear is not even. Normally, there will be grooves worn into the surfaces. Wear also results in a very high polish on the metal surfaces. Heat can produce some warping of the metal parts. All of these are undesirable and diminish the effectiveness of the brakes. By turning the rotors and drums in a special lathe, the mechanic can usually restore the metal surface to nearly new condition. It is my belief and the recommendation of the mechanics I talked with that rotors and drums should always be turned. The expense is minimal.

REPAIR OR REPLACE?

Sometimes wear is so severe that turning is not practical. That can be the case with a severely warped or grooved rotor or drum. In that case, the only alternative is replacement with a new part. The need for replacement can be reduced by being aware of how your brakes are functioning and having them checked at any indication of unusual noises or braking action.

Brake cylinders are the mechanical parts that force the shoes or pads against the metal parts. In tow vehicles and smaller motorhomes, the pedal pressure is transferred by hydraulic pressure through the master cylinder and brake lines to the wheel cylinders. The pressure causes a piston in each cylinder to move and forces the friction materials against the rotor or drum. Whenever there is movement of mechanical parts, there is always some wear. Eventually, the wear becomes sufficient to warrant repair and/or replacement.

Too, hydraulic brake fluid tends to absorb moisture. The brake system is only partially sealed from the air. Whenever the supply of fluid is checked at the master cylinder, some air and moisture enter the system. That can of fluid you keep to top off the system collects air and moisture every time you open it. The moisture collects in larger and larger drops in the fluid and, being heavier than the hydraulic fluid, drifts to the bottom of the system. That happens to be the wheel cylinders. Once in the wheel cylinders, the moisture causes the metal parts of the cylinder to rust. The rust wears the seals on the pistons and they begin to leak. It's a mess. The rule is to have the cylinders on drum brakes reconditioned every time the shoes are replaced.

The situation with disc brakes on your front wheels is different. The rust develops there, too, but in that case the rubber seals don't move and develop leaks. So that isn't usually a problem. Also, the disc brake pistons don't have the same amount of travel as the rear brake pistons. They are not moving constantly over that rough surface.

But the calipers -- those parts which apply pressure to the rotors -- can get very rusty. This is especially true if you live in the northern part of the country where huge amounts of salt are applied to your car every winter. That rust may build up to the point that the calipers can't move freely. It doesn't always happen. My experts both said 90 per cent of the time, front disc brake actuating systems would not need servicing. Leave it to your mechanic.

Another question that comes up at brake repair time relates to the type of friction materials to use. Until recently, asbestos was almost universally the material of choice. It had superior reactions to heat, gave relatively long life, and was gentle on the metal parts. But asbestos has been found to be severely carcinogenic when the dust is inhaled. In spite of all precautions mechanics can reasonably take, inhaling some of the dust is unavoidable. Asbestos is being phased out of use in brakes. Various other products are being used in combinations.

But even before we learned it was dangerous, we discovered that asbestos was less than satisfactory in some brake installations. When asbestos gets hot, it tends to lose some of its friction. This can happen at high vehicle speeds or with repeated braking such as coming down maountains or with heavy loads. Many different attempts have been made to counteract these problems by using fillers such as limestone and clay and various metal powders.

Another approach is to use very high temperatures to melt various kinds of metallic powders together to form a product called sintered metal. Sintered metal brakes have superior resistence to heat and longer wear. But there are compromises: They tend to be noisy, wear the brake drums rapidly and have very low stopping ability until warmed up. Most experienced drivers with sintered metal brakes ride the pedal for a few minutes when they first start in order to warm up the brakes.

Another material which has become very popular is made by pressing various fibers and metallic powders with bonding agents in molds under very high pressure. The result is semi-metallic brake material. Since semi-metallic has friction characteristics superior to asbestos and does not degrade the brake drums and rotors as rapidly as sintered metal, it is becoming widely used.

With all these choices, guess what I was told when I asked for a recommendation on materials. The manufacturers and the brake specialists all said, "Use the same materials originally used on your vehicle." I find that a less than satisfactory answer because I know that manufacturers like to use the least expensive product that will give just acceptable performance.

From what I've been able to learn about the various products, I would ask for semi-metallic for my breakes if it is available. If not, I would ask for the best possible quality organic materials.

Brake materials are no place to save money by buying bargain-priced parts. The lives of you and your family depend on the ability to stop your rig safely. The difference between cheap and top quality parts is so small as to make the cheap ones no bargain. Buy high quality, heavy-duty brake pads and shoes.

Okay, now assume that you've got your brakes installed. There is one more thing that needs to be considered. Brakes must be broken in properly. Too many drivers with a new brake job run up to 70 mph and stomp on the brakes to see if the mechanic did it right. He could have used the best materials and precision labor, and those brakes will be headed down the drain anyway. For the first 200 miles, brakes should be used lightly. They are never shaped to fit the brake drums and rotors precisely. Light application for a couple of hundred miles permits the high spots to wear down and shape to fit. Heavy pressure and the resulting high heat on high spots of brand new brakes glaze the materials. The result is less than satisfactory brakes and noise. Break them in.

BRAKES FOR TRAILERS

Most trailer brakes operate by converting the pedal pressure of the tow vehicle into electrical energy. The electrical energy powers an electromagnet at each wheel. The magnet is attached to an arm or lever. When the magnet is energized, it is drawn to an iron ring or armature attached to the trailer wheel. The magnet tries to follow the armature but can't. But in trying to follow, it forces the brake shoe against the brake drum. The action is very similar to the braking action of the drum brakes on the rear wheels of the tow vehicle.

However, the braking action of the trailer brakes is seldom as smooth and controlled as the braking action of the tow vehicle. This results in wear patterns that are different. Trailer brakes need more frequent inspection. It is probably a good idea to check your trailer brakes every 10,000 miles. Trailer brakes are somewhat simpler to inspect and repair, and most owners can do it themselves if they aren't afraid of getting a bit messy.

Check for the usual things such as grooving, rust, uneven wear patterns and badly worn friction material. Check whether the magnet is wearing evenly across its face. If it isn't, it needs to be replaced. You also must determine the cause of the unevenness. Usually the problem is a worn lever pin that permits the magnet lever to wobble. In that case, replace the lever assembly.

Also check the surface of the armature the magnet rubs against. Some grooving is normal and of little concern, but severe wear is cause for replacement. If you need to replace the magnet on one wheel, you should also replace the magnet on the wheel on the other end of that axle to produce even braking action.

Since trailer brakes are electrically operated, you also need to inspect the corresponding electrical lines and connections periodically. Be sure all connections are clean and tight. All electric lines should be secured to prevent rubbing of the insulation or snagging. Any lines that indicate possible worn insulation should be replaced. There should be grommets or similar devices to prevent chaffing at any point that wires go through holes in either metal or wood.

SELECTING A MECHANIC

Earlier I promised to give suggestions on selecting a mechanic you can trust. A system that works well for me is to go to a few large parts stores and ask for the names of the best mechanics in town. Soon, you will start hearing the same names mentioned. Visit the shops of these men or women. Without getting in the way, look around. A good mechanic will have a shop that is clean and free of debris. His tools will be clean and organized. He will frequently wipe the dirt and grease from his hands. He will wipe the dirt from parts before he removes them so that the dirt can't contaminate other parts.

Ask a few intelligent questions and listen carefully. Don't expect him to give you step by step instructions on how to make a repair, but he shouldn't try to hide behind mechanical double-talk. When you find one of these paragons, nurture him. Pay his fair bill without quibbling. Listen to his explanations and suggestions, and don't be afraid to ask questions. But don't get in his way. No mechanic will ever get wealthy from doing repair work. It's a tough business made tougher by clients who want to stick their noses into the works or "help."

One of the worst frights an RVer can have is for his brakes to fail coming down a mountain. That's the stuff of nightmares. Having an understanding of how your brakes work and how to keep them working can help to change the nightmare into a pleasant dream.

Chapter 6

By the Numbers For Safety

Ever wonder what would happen if your trailer came loose? At 60 mph? On a busy road? Me, too. Nightmares are made of such stuff. I didn't get to see it happen, but my dad's trailer somehow came loose about 40 years ago. I have his word for it that there was lots of noise and an adrenalin rush. But Dad was lucky. He had done at least one thing right.

There are lots of adventures and misadventures in RVing. Some of the misadventures can be avoided with some simple procedures. That's what this chapter is about.

I used to fly a lot. One of the things that are drilled into all would-be birdmen is the absolute necessity of following procedures. One example is keeping your mind completely on what you're doing when landing. Once I had started my landing procedures, there was no sound in the plane other than the rushing wind and the engine. No conversation. None. There may have been occasional gasps from one of the rear seats, but there were no questions and no answers. Flying is life's second greatest thrill. (If I have to remind you of the first greatest, you've been talking sometime when you should have been paying attention to procedures.) But flying is not much fun if you have to buy another airplane after each landing.

In RVing, there are several instances when conversation would better be avoided. One is hitching up time. It is too easy to let yourself become distracted and leave out an important step. Such as closing the ball latch.

ROUTINE FOR HOOKUP

Every trailerist should establish very early in his trailering career a routine for hitching up. Then don't let the routine vary. Don't stop to answer questions. Don't become a referee between the kids and the dog. And if anything does unavoidably divert your attention, start over. Check every step.

Here's what I do. Once the truck is backed into position, I lower the trailer until the weight is solidly on the ball. Then close the latch. Then I crank the trailer up several turns. That makes it a little easier to attach the spring bars. More importantly, it shows that the trailer is firmly attached to the truck. Then I attach the spring bars. I don't have to worry about whether I have used the proper link because when I first set up the hitch and trailer, I marked the correct links with a piece of insulated wire.

Then I raise the jack completely. That's important. Some owners raise the jack only a short distance. Sooner or later, they are going to go over a ridge or bump, wipe out the bottom of the jackpost and be in the market for a new jack. Raise that sucker all the way. Next, I place the block I use for a jack pad in the truck. I'll need it again.

Then I hook up the electrical cord to the truck, hook up the breakaway switch and install the safety chains. Finally, I inspect everything.

BREAKAWAY SWITCH & CHAINS

Notice that I don't hook up the breakaway switch until after the trailer is on the ball. A lot of owners loop the cable from the breakaway switch over the ball. I don't think that's a good idea. A ball shank rarely breaks, but the next one that does won't be the first one. If the ball shank breaks and the cable is attached to the ball, what is going to activate the breakaway switch? You're right. Nothing. Hook the cable to something else.

Notice, too, that I hooked up the safety chains. That's the thing Dad did right. As a result, he took some paint off the underside of the A-frame, bent the jackpost and raised his attention level, but he didn't lose the trailer.

Had that happened to a guy I know, the trailer would have been destroyed. And someone may have been killed. This friend hooks his chains in such a way that if the trailer should ever come loose, the chains will break loose too, and let 6,000 pounds of trailer go its merry way. That is extreme irresponsibility. It's also very illegal.

Let me state very clearly: You have a responsibility for that trailer. If it comes loose, you are responsible for where it goes and what it does. Safety chains work. They protect innocent people from becoming statistics. They even save trailers.

On to some other items of procedure. Ever had the refrigerator door come open while you're merrily tooling down the way? Ever had a dozen eggs and a six-pack dump on the floor? I have. Once. That was enough. I'll blame it on my fishing buddy, but it was still my RV, and I should have checked. It wouldn't have happened if I had used a check list.

USE THE CHECK LIST

That's another thing airplane pilots learn very early. Use the check list. Every time. You should have a check list, too. Make your own. List on it everything that needs to be done before the trailer is moved. Doors should be latched. All of them. The refrigerator should be locked. The furnace turned off. Ditto the water heater. Turn off the water pump. Close the windows and vents. Lower the TV antenna. Secure everything that isn't in a cabinet. Turn off the refrigerator burner. What? You don't? More about that in a moment.

Lock the door. Stow the step. Put away the water hose. Finally, as you drive away, look back to see if there is anything you left. Whoops! There comes the electric power post. You forgot the power cord. Add it to the check list.

Now about that refrigerator. Down the road a few miles, you're going to need some gas. In spite of all you do to be careful, some gas fumes are going to get away. Or someone else will spill some gas. All it takes to make a tragedy is for some of that gasoline vapor to drift into the outer vent on your refrigerator, reach the flame, and your insurance company will rebuild the station. You might even get another RV if you live.

Turn off the burner. Modern refrigerators are wonderful devices. They will hold the contents of a well-chilled refrigerator to a safe temperature for several hours with the burner off. If you feel you just can't leave the burner off, at least stop a few miles ahead and turn it off. Then wait until you have left the station before relighting.

Hal and Penny Gaynor, who write the column "RV Safety Clinic," feel so strongly about the danger of a refrigerator-induced fire that they refuse to pull into a filling station if there is another RV fueling. They are right.

Procedures for doing things are not always fun. Eggs and beer on the carpet aren't any fun, either. Neither is a trailer coming off the hitch. Following procedures can help us avoid those misadventures.

Chapter 7

Engine Heat... How to Deal With It

Now's a good time to think about all the heat you had to deal with last summer and figure out what to do about it. There are at least three kinds of heat that cause trouble in an RV -- engine, engine oil and transmission heat. Some is necessary, but too much is trouble.

Excess heat can be more than just uncomfortable; it can destroy your engine or transmission. Some 23% of gasoline energy is released into the cooling system of your engine. From there it passes into the air. A major problem can occur if the transfer isn't satisfactory.

An engine needs to run fairly hot to be efficient. Fuel is burned more completely in a hot engine. Various contaminants migrate to the engine oil. If the engine does not develop enough heat to boil off those contaminants, they convert into acids and sludge. Neither is healthful for an engine.

To make sure the engine does warm up rapidly and maintain an even operating temperature, engineers install a thermostat. Most thermostats used today are set at 195 degrees. That's hotter than needed, but the government has said that installing a cooler-temperature thermostat is illegal. Unless you can find a wrench the right size, you can't change it. Finding the right wrench should take you all of two minutes. Then buy a 180-degree thermostat. If you need more heat in the winter, change back to the 195 for cold weather. That's what I do. Just don't fall for the old myth that an engine will run cooler with no thermostat. Some engines will actually run hotter. None will run well unless the temperature is kept to about 180 degrees.

BOOST COOLING ABILITY

Many trailer towers are pulling with cars and trucks that were originally purchased to move passengers or a light load. Their cooling systems weren't designed for 10,000 pounds or more. Consider having your radiator recored. Any radiator shop can build you a radiator with more tubes using your present top and bottom tanks. You need at least four rows of tubes in an RV, or for towing one. Some trucks can also utilize a radiator that is wider than the original. I don't believe it's possible to install too much cooling capacity for RVing.

A lot of heat is generated in an automatic transmission. All automatics come with some cooling capacity built into the bottom of the radiator. Salespersons are fond of assuring anyone who asks that they don't need more. When one tells you that, just smile and go buy a large auxiliary cooler. When transmission fluid hits a temperature above 250 degrees, it begins to oxidize. Oxidized fluid not only loses its ability to lubricate, but it also becomes abrasive. Continued operation with oxidized transmission fluid leads to an expensive repair. Check yours occasionally if you think it might have been running too hot. If it's not red, it's not good.

Every RV needs an auxiliary transmission cooler. How big? Here is one place where bigger is definitely better. You can't get transmission fluid too cool. Most cooler manufacturers rate their coolers for a maximum number of pounds of vehicle. Compute your worst case of combined load and add at least 50%. Doubling would be even better. Mount your cooler in front of the radiator or air conditioner condenser if you can. If necessary, it's all right to mount the cooler at an angle in the space below the radiator. Keep it out of the way of flying rocks. If you're concerned about its being out of the airstream, get an electric radiator fan for the cooler.

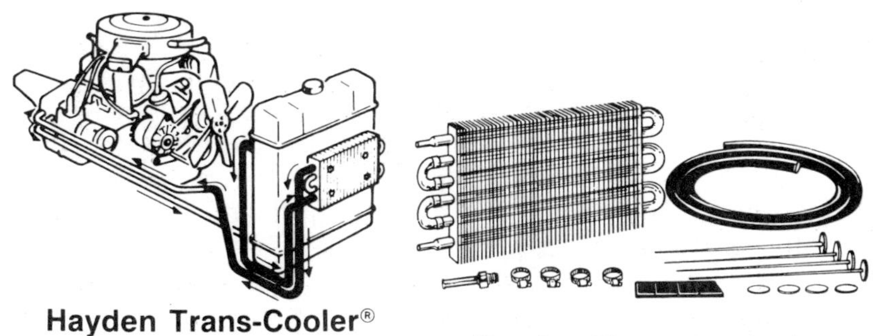

Hayden Trans-Cooler®
In-Series Installation

Hayden Trans-Cooler®

ENGINE OIL COOLERS

There are minor discussions about how to hook up the lines to the cooler. I prefer to have the fluid run through the auxiliary cooler first and then through the built-in cooler. There is no reason to omit the built-in cooler.

Some owners ask about using engine oil coolers. It's true that some engines do generate high temperatures in the oil. Oil does a lot more than just make things slippery. The oil is an important part of the cooling system. It would seem to make sense to add some sort of oil cooler, but in most cases it isn't necessary. Engine oil is made to run hot. If it doesn't reach and maintain temperatures of around 220 degrees, it can't boil off the contaminants. Too much cooling would be detrimental. Most engines don't need additional engine oil cooling. If you think yours does, be very sure to get a cooler with a built-in thermostat. Otherwise, you can cool the oil too much.

One of the things an engine does best is generate heat. About 60% of the energy in every gallon of gasoline you burn goes into wasted heat. A little over half of that goes out the exhaust pipe. There's not much we can do about the exhaust heat. Fuel has to be burned to produce energy. At the present time, internal combustion engines aren't capable of converting all of that heat energy to mechanical energy. One thing we can do is make the exhaust heat more bearable.

An unfortunate fact of RV life is that the exhaust system runs under the passenger area. On a day with an ambient temperature of 95 degrees, we don't need that exhaust heat boiling up through the floor to tell us it's hot. Motorhome and truck designers haven't done a very good job of baffling that heat out. Building a baffle out of sheet aluminum placed between the exhaust pipes and the RV floor would help a lot. About 34% of energy in a gallon of fuel ends up in the exhaust system. Anything that will keep it from coming into the passenger compartment is a help. Just keep the baffle from touching the exhaust system and try to have some moving air between the baffle and the floor.

There's a lot of heat around any engine. It's unavoidable. The best we can do is find ways to minimize the negative effects with exhaust baffling and adequate cooling systems.

Chapter 8

Fire Extinguishers May Cost You Your Life

Suppose you were to awaken in the predawn darkness tomorrow morning to the screaming of your smoke detector. As the sound and sight of flames greet your shocked mind, what price would you pay for a good fire extinguisher? Your RV is going up in flames. Would a good fire extinguisher be worth $50? $100? Never mind. You're about to settle for that $5 wonder hanging over by the door. And the chances are excellent that it will cost you and your insurance company the price of a new RV plus all of those priceless personal possessions. And maybe someone's life.

The sad fact is that most fire extinguishers in RVs are nearly worthless. They are disposable extinguishers, and that's what should be done with them. Dispose of them. That's the information gleaned from interviews with two chiefs of fire departments and a long-time dealer in firefighting equipment.

Another sad fact is that most of us give no thought about the effectiveness of the fire extinguisher in our RV. We know dimly that there is one over by the door and that you sorta aim it at the fire and pull a trigger, or press a button, or something. We may have from $5,000 to $500,000 invested in the RV and $5 invested in the sole means of protecting it from fire. We'll spend additional hundreds of dollars on stereos, televisions, antennas, microwaves and other gadgets and expect to protect it all with a $5 plastic bottle hanging by the door that we haven't even looked at since we bought the RV five years ago.

So what's wrong with the $5 wonder? If it's no good, why did the manufacturer put it there? Good questions. In reverse order, the manufacturer included a fire extinguisher because he was legally required to do it. The reason he included that one is that he couldn't find a cheaper one. He knows that fire extinguishers don't sell RVs. He knows that most of us couldn't care less about the little red thing down by the door.

Now, what's wrong with it? For one thing, it's too small. For another, there is often no way of knowing whether it will work when needed. Let's look at the different types of fires, how fire extinguishers work, and how they are made.

THREE TYPES OF RV FIRES

There are three common types of fires, and all three are likelv to occur in an RV. Class A fires are fires composed of ordinary combustible materials such as paper, wood, textiles, plastic and rubber. There are a lot of those kinds of materials in any RV. Class B fires involve burning liquids such as motor fuel, cooking oils and propane. Some of that is usually found in RVs. Class C fires involve electricity. A short circuit or overheated electrical appliance would be part of a Class C fire. As you can readily see, any fire in an RV might involve all three groups.

The importance of recognizing the type of fire becomes apparent when you consider that the same firefighting techniques can't be used on all three types. To cite a common problem, water is an effective tool against Class A fires. But water only spreads Class B fires by floating the burning material on top of the fire. And using water on a Class C fire would likely lead to electrocution of the firefighter.

Since fire requires three things -- fuel, oxygen and heat -- the methods of fighting fires involve attempting to remove one or more of the elements. For example, using water on a Class A fire lowers the temperature of the fuel below that required for combustion and seals off the fuel from oxygen. A frequent suggestion for a small Class A or

B fire is to smother it by throwing a rug or heavy blanket over it. This seals out the oxygen and stops the fire. Commonly used fire extinguishers employ some chemical selected to accomplish the same thing.

Any fire extinguisher selected for an RV should be designed to fight all three types of fires. There are three basic types of extinguishers, classified according to the active material they contain. One is the carbon dioxide (CO) extinguisher which floods the fire with a blanket of carbon dioxide, smothering the fire. These can be quite effective on indoor Class B and C fires, but they lose effectiveness rapidly when used outdoors. Carbon dioxide is very lightweight, and any breeze easily blows it away from the fire.

The most frequently used material in fire extinguishers is a dry powder of ammonium phosphate. When applied to a fire, ammonium phosphate releases gases and residue that smother the fire as does carbon dioxide. Being heavier, it is not so easily blown away. Another dry chemical, sodium bicarbonate, is frequently recommended for a fire extinguisher used primarily in kitchens because it is more effective on grease fires. Both materials are effective on Class B and C fires but less so on Class A fires. But the biggest drawback to either is that the residue they leave behind is messy and corrosive.

WHAT ABOUT HALON?

Halon gas is often used to fight fires where the lack of residue can be important. Fires around technical equipment such as computers is one example where halon is superior. Halon extinguishers carry ratings for both Class B and C fires. Like dry chemical extinguishers, halon is less effective against Class A fires. A major problem with halon is that it has been found to deplete the Earth's ozone layer seriously. Recently, several nations, including the United States, agreed to freeze halon production at 1986 levels as a way of protecting against future environmental damage.

Until other chemicals are developed to fight fires, the dry extinguisher seems to be the best choice. As one fire chief said, "I tell people to fight the fire and then worry about the residue. If you don't put out the fire, it makes no difference whether there is any residue."

But if most fire extinguishers use the same dry chemicals, why does it make any difference whether one costs $5 or $50? Well, so far we've looked at the types of fires and the chemicals used to fight them. The job of the fire extinguisher is to store the material until needed and then direct it forcefully to the base of the fire. Not all similar-appearing devices do that equally well.

The dry chemical is stored in the extinguisher with some inert gas -- usually either nitrogen or carbon dioxide -- under high pressure. When a valve is released, the rushing gas siphons the powder out of the extinguisher and blows it forcefully out of the nozzle. The siphon tube is mounted in the control head of the extinguisher and reaches to near the bottom of the container. With many inexpensive extinguishers, the siphon tube can fall out of the head and you will never know it. When you open the valve to fight a fire, all you get is a whoosh from the gas, no chemical.

EXTINGUISHER PROBLEMS

Another problem with inexpensive extinguishers is that the pressure gauge -- if there even is one -- is simply clipped into position and sealed with an "O" ring. If the plastic head or the gauge stem should happen to be a less than perfect fit, the propellant gas would leak out and you would never know it. When you pull the trigger, you won't even get a whoosh.

Better-quality extinguishers use control heads made of metal with siphon tubes and gauges that are securely screwed into place. This type construction makes it less likely that the extinguisher will ask "Say wha'?" when you pull the trigger to fight your fire. They can also be recharged after use. Some inexpensive extinguishers cannot and you may not know it. The differences are worth considering.

Fire extinguishers come in several sizes with ratings to match. Ratings for commonly used extinguishers run from 1 to 40. The ratings indicate the size of the fire with which the extinguisher has been tested as effective. Larger numbers are more effective. But larger numbers also indicate a bulkier extinguisher. The two fire chiefs who were queried agreed that an RV should have an extinguisher rated at least 2A:20B:C and that most RVs should have two.

Where the extinguisher is located is important. It should be readily available and not likely to be damaged by casual traffic. The normal location near the main door is excellent. That way it can be reached from outside the RV with minimal exposure to any fire that may be raging inside. Trailerists should have a second extinguisher in the tow vehicle.

LEARN HOW TO USE EXTINGUISHERS

It shouldn't be necessary to state the obvious, but all older members of the family should be familiar with the operation of the extinguisher(s). Children should also be taught that extinguishers are not toys and are never handled except to check their condition and to fight a fire. Checking condition is important. Never own an extinguisher that doesn't have a gauge indicating the amount of pressure inside. Check the gauge regularly to be sure it is still up to operating pressure. If it isn't, have it recharged immediately. When a fire breaks out, you will be too busy doing other things to worry about getting the extinguisher recharged.

Some people either don't know or forget how to use an extinguisher. Immediately upon removing it from its mounting clip, remove the safety pin. Move as close to the fire as you safely can. Aim the nozzle at the base of the fire and activate the device. Continue operation until the fire is completely out. Stand by for further operation if it should become necessary. Then get the extinguisher recharged immediately.

All firefighting experts agree on one other procedure. Have a plan and be certain everyone knows it. The first thing to do when the smoke alarm sounds -- you do have one, don't you? -- is to get everybody out of the RV. Get the younger members of the family well away from danger. Then one adult should begin operation of the extinguisher while another shuts off the propane tanks. Next, that person or another old enough to do so should run for help. Someone should make an effort to get the tow vehicle away from the trailer. The electric cord should also be jerked loose from the electric pole before anyone tries to use any water on the fire. Use no water if there are any burning liquids until that portion of the fire is safely out and there is no possibility of water spreading the liquid to other burning areas.

Most of us tend to procrastinate. Getting adequate fire extinguishers is not the place to procrastinate. Nor is it the place to economize. The $5 wonder you got with the RV isn't enough. Ask yourself the question that was raised at the beginning of this article. Then spend enough money now to get the appropriate extinguisher. We all hope you never need it.

Chapter 9

Fuel Injectors, Carburetors and RVs

Very shortly all new tow vehicle and motorhome engines will come equipped with some sort of fuel injection. Owners will have to become familiar with such things as throttle body injectors, multi-port injectors, electronic fuel injection, and similar terms non-existent only a few years ago. Gone will be carburetors as we knew them.

The results of using fuel injection are debatable. Engines start and run more smoothly. Throttle response may be improved. Power may be increased. And emissions are reduced. That's the plus side. Some engineers maintain that equal power and smoothness could be obtained with better use of carburetor and manifold technology. That will be argued for years. What is known for sure is that injector technology delivers most of what it promises over a longer life than carburetors. But when the little black box quits, that's all she wrote. You don't limp home. You stay where you are until someone brings in the repair parts. At least with carburetors, you could make it home.

Never mind. We have a few choices. We can opt for older equipment with carburetors. We can buy diesels, most of which have mechanically controlled injector systems. Or we can learn as much as possible about the new injector technology before making our selection of new equipment. That's what this chapter is about. What are the new systems, who builds them, what are the differences, what do you do when they lunch themselves?

We need a little background in fuel systems and operation so that we can understand why and what fuel injectors do. If an internal combustion engine is to run efficiently, it must receive proper amounts of air and fuel in the right place at the right time. The right place is the engine cylinder between the top of the piston and the cylinder head. The proper time is before the piston reaches the top of its stroke as the fuel/air mixture is compressed. Let's just deal with the air for a moment.

THE IDEAL CONDITION

Ideally, the engine would consume a cylinder full of air with each intake and compression stroke. That is, if each cylinder had a volume of 60 cubic inches, it would fill with exactly 60 cubic inches of air each time.

That seldom happens. As the piston rushes down on the intake stroke, pressure within the cylinder is less than the surrounding pressure of the air. The outside air tries to fill this area of low pressure, and it would if it had time. But the filling time is short and there are lots of impediments in the way. First there is the air cleaner that removes all the dirt and bugs and other unwanted materials. The air cleaner acts as a restriction to air flow. Next there is a carburetor or some other fuel mixing device and a throttle valve. The purpose of the throttle valve is to control the amount of air that gets to the cylinder. More air usually equals more power. We don't always want to be generating full power. All of this acts as more restriction.

The purpose of the carburetor or other mixing device is to add exactly the proper amount of fuel for the amount of air that is allowed to pass. It, too, adds its restriction. Finally, the mixture passes through the intake manifold to the cylinders. If there is only one cylinder, the intake manifold is quite simple. Most engines have multiple cylinders. The more cylinders, the more complicated is the manifold with all of its twists and turns with arms of differing lengths.

TURNS IN THE MANIFOLD

Here in the manifold is where some of the worst damage to smooth-running, powerful engines develops. Building a manifold with exactly equal length runners to each cylinder is the ideal but, given the restrictions of space and materials, it is nearly impossible. Designing a manifold with runners without turns is equally impossible. The problem with turns in a manifold is that the fuel particles tend to skid out on the turns and find a lodging place on the sides of the manifold.

Too, the air-fuel mixture tends to cool slightly as it passes through the manifold. Some of the fuel particles condense and fall out of the mixture. In either case, some cylinders get more fuel with each intake stroke than do others. Some cylinders will have a lean mixture and some will have a rich mixture. Some may even get an ideal mixture.

That's part of the problem with using a carburetor. Fuel is mixed with air before it enters the manifold. Cylinders get unequal mixtures and unequal amounts. The result is an engine that runs slightly rough and develops less power than its capabilities.

There are other problems. The velocity of air through the carburetor and manifold varies fantastically as the engine speed and power requirements vary. The ability of the carburetor to furnish a proper fuel-air mixture also varies with the air velocity. Government-mandated emissions and mileage requirements have complicated the task. Carburetor and manifold designers have done a fantastic job working out the compromises, but compromises must always be there.

THE FUEL INJECTOR

Enter the fuel injector. The fuel injector with its attendant electronics replaces the most complicated portion of the carburetor, the metering section. Injectors have been used in diesel engines for decades, but the ones used in gasoline engines are both similar and different. Some car manufacturers, mostly European, have tried for many years to design an efficient injector system. The problem has always been one of balancing the amount of fuel with the amount of air. Now that nearly all car and truck gasoline engines are computer-controlled the solution has been found.

There are two main injector systems used. All gasoline engines use a throttle body. This is simply a butterfly valve that is actuated by accelerator pedal pressure and controls the amount of air entering the engine. One type of injector is located as part of the throttle body and is usually referred to as a throttle-body injector or single-point injector. The other injector system uses an injector for each cylinder located in the intake manifold as close as possible to the cylinder. This is usually called a multi-point or multi-port system.

In truck engines, Ford has chosen the multi-port system. General Motors has elected to use the throttle-body system. Dodge has been late in making the shift to an injector system but appears to have decided to go with throttle-body injectors for most of its truck engines. Since the throttle-body system is located where the carburetor used to be, all of the problems of fuel fall-out in the intake manifold still exist. In effect, the throttle-body injector becomes a computer-controlled carburetor.

Both systems are controlled by computers. Individual designs vary, but factors that can be used to determine the amount of fuel are engine speed, manifold pressure, engine temperature, air charge temperature, throttle position, exhaust gas recirculation, exhaust gas temperature and crankshaft rotation location. Each of these has a sensor that feeds information to the computer. (I would not be surprised to find a sensor measuring the level of anxiety of the driver in next year's models.)

COMPUTER IS THE KEY

When all of the factors above are read by the computer, it sends a signal to the injector to squirt the required amount of fuel into the intake air stream. With an eight-cylinder engine running at 3000 rpm. the computer is giving 12,000 commands per minute. But, remember, there are thousands of other decisions being made for each command. Without the computer to control the system, it could never work.

The results have been engines that start faster, run more smoothly, sometimes develop greater power and torque, produce higher fuel mileage, and emit fewer air pollutants. We ought to be happy, and most of us are. But there are problems with any complicated mechanical and electrical system, and some RVers are concerned.

For example, many RVers drive their rigs miles back into the boonies. What would happen if the injector system failed fifty miles off the main road? For that matter, what happens when an injector system fails and how reliable is it?

Well, carburetors develop troubles, too. Most of us have experienced carburetor problems. But sudden, total death of a carburetor is an extremely rare event. They usually give clear warning of trouble with the difficulty increasing in severity over an extended period of time. We can always limp home with an ailing carburetor.

SUDDEN DEATH

Not so with an injector. When an injector quits, it quits. There is seldom any warning and there is little, if anything, you can do to fix it yourself. To find out what happens and how frequently, I talked with independent mechanics and a dealer service manager. What I found out is both encouraging and somewhat alarming.

Throttle-body injectors often depend upon one injector. When it goes, your engine is dead. According to my mechanic, there is seldom any warning. When I asked him what he would do if he was going to drive a throttle-body engine into the boonies, he said he would carry a spare injector. The cost? A new throttle-body injector costs about $140. How does that grab you? My mechanic suggested buying a used one. The price would be much less. If you take that route, I suggest you be sure and have the appropriate repair manual and tools with you. But you do that anyway, don't you?

With multi-port injectors, the situation is different. You have eight injectors instead of one. If one fails, you still have seven cylinders to get you home. Can you replace one under a tree? The local Ford service manager said, "Probably not. Unless you have had the course, you'll probably break the old injector trying to get it out."

How often can you expect trouble? All my sources agreed that injectors are more reliable than carburetors. They agreed, too, that there are some things you can do to improve your chances of not having a failure. The main cause of injector failure seems to be bad fuel. Not contaminated fuel; fuel filters are very efficient at removing dirt. The problem is that some brands of gasoline don't contain detergents. Some of the additives in gasoline tend to clog the tiny openings in the injectors. When they are clogged, your engine quits. The moral is clear: Use gasoline that contains a detergent.

I was still concerned about the electronics. What happens when the computer quits? The Ford service manager said that he could not remember ever having an engine with a total computer failure. The usual problem was glitches that caused hard starting or rough running enough to warn the most obtuse driver that there were problems. Perhaps.

INJECTORS ARE HERE TO STAY

There is one thing clear. Until a better engine or fuel system is developed, we are going to find fuel injectors and complicated electronic control systems in our motorhomes and tow vehicles. The improved engine performance is impressive. The problems are infrequent.

However, the power increases are illusory. For example, in comparing the carbureted versions of Ford 302 and 351 engines with their injected counterparts, it appears that the injected models develop greatly increased power. And they do. What isn't shown is that Ford stubbornly continued using two-barrel carburetors on these engines. Two-barrel carburetors don't permit engines to develop their full potential. In Ford's case, the power increases were to a large extent due to improved breathing capacity.

It seems to me there are three things we can do. We can decide which of the injector systems is more appealing and learn to live with it. For a while, we can drive older models with carburetors. Or we can get a diesel engine. Each answer has its advantages and disadvantages. Wouldn't you know it? The problem is still yours.

	Carbureted Version		Injected Version	
	Horsepower	Torque	Horsepower	Torque
Ford 302	150	250	185	270
Ford 351	190	285	210	315
Ford 460	245	380	Not available yet	
Chevy 305	160	250	170	235
Chevy 350	165	275	210	300
Chevy 454	230	370	230	385

Horsepower and torque figures will vary somewhat according to the application as will the speeds at which each is developed. However, the relationships between sizes of engines will remain close.

Chapter 10

Gear Down With A Different Gear Set

Selecting gear ratios for RVs would be simple if we had to consider only one set of conditions. It would be easy to select proper gearing for cruising or for climbing and acceleration. Unfortunately, we have to deal with both. That calls for compromises. The best gear ratio for cruising may not be best for climbing and acceleration. The reverse is also true.

Modern transmissions do a fantastic job of dealing with the compromises. The new five-speed manuals are an excellent example. With those trannies, there is a gear for just about any condition you could imagine. The large automatics are also excellent under most conditions. With gear ratios of 2.46 and 1.46 in first and second gear, respectively, the torque converter combines to give most RVers good performance for climbing and acceleration when used with a final gear ratio in the rear end that is suitable for cruising.

But, predictably, not everyone is happy with those gears. I've recently been getting mail from owners who say, "My gearing is great for cruising on fairly level road, but it takes forever to reach cruising speed. And climbing steep grades is painful. I don't want to change the rear end gearing, but is there something else I can do?" Now there is.

In fact, there are three things that can be done. I have previously written about overdrives and underdrives. One of those can be an answer for some folk but not for all. There are two other solutions that might be better for RVers such as the example mentioned earlier.

John Kilgore (412 S. San Fernando Blvd., Burbank, CA 91502) has a couple of kits for modifications to the automatics we commonly use, the Ford C-6 and GM Turbo 400-475. These are excellent transmissions in stock condition. But some owners would like slightly lower gearing in first and second gears. Kilgore has two answers.

TRY A HIGHER STALL SPEED

One answer is to change the torque converter to one with a higher stall speed. Torque converters give additional torque when climbing and accelerating by allowing varying amounts of slippage. This permits the engine to run faster at the same road speed. Normally, higher engine speeds translate to higher torque and more power. The effect is the same as a continuous series of lower gears. As road speed increases, slippage decreases. The torque converter stops slipping entirely at some engine speed. That speed is called the torque converter's stall speed. The higher the stall speed, the greater the slippage and the greater the climbing power and acceleration.

Torque converters with high stall speed are good for climbing and accelerating, but they are less than satisfactory for cruising. Torque converter slippage generates heat in the transmission and costs fuel mileage. Kilgore handles that problem by making a two-speed torque converter actuated by an electric switch. In one position, you have a torque converter with a high stall speed. A second position gives a low stall speed for cruise conditions. (A third position, "auto," shifts to high stall when the brakes are applied. As soon as the brakes are released, it switches back to low stall. This position is intended to eliminate transmission creep at stop lights.)

Sounds good, but I'm afraid of it. If the driver forgets to switch to normal operation, the torque converter continues its high stall speed mode and generates lots of heat. Also, if used in high stall speed for climbing a mountain -- a situation where it would be of help -- it generates lots of heat at the very time the RV is having heat troubles enough. Kilgore has another answer that I like better.

He also has a replacement planetary gear set with lower ratios in first and second gears. Third gear remains the same as stock. First gear becomes 2.75 instead of the 2.46 in Fords and 2.48 in GMs. That's a 12% or 11% increase in torque. Second gear becomes 1.57 instead of the 1.46 in Fords and 1.48 in GMs for a 7% or 6% increase in torque. These changes give better acceleration without increasing torque converter heat. Climbing in the two lower gears will also be improved without increasing transmission heat.

RPMs ARE INCREASED

Theoretically, the transmission should run a bit cooler when climbing because there is less slippage from the torque converter than with stock gears. As an example, if your engine turns 2800 rpm at a road speed of 50 mph in second gear now, with Kilgore's gear set, it would turn 2996 rpm. The engine is running faster and developing more horsepower, which means it is pulling a lower vacuum and not working as hard.

A transmission with Kilgore's gear set becomes a wide ratio instead of a narrow ratio transmission. That simply means that the steps between gears are wider than in a narrow ratio tranny. Because of their wide torque curve, gasoline engines work well with wide ratio transmissions. The opposite is true of most diesels. Most diesels have a very narrow torque band. That's why big diesel trucks have so many gears. They need to match road speed to engine speed more carefully than do drivers of gasoline engines.

Even though the new GM and Ford diesels operate at engine speeds only dreamed of by heavy duty diesels, they still have torque curves more narrow than gasoline engines.

I expected to find that rpm drop on shifts from first to second and second to third would be too wide for efficient operation with the wide ratio transmission. The drops are somewhat greater than with the narrow box, but don't appear to be excessive. Diesel operators might simply find that they need to accelerate to slightly higher road speeds before making their gear shifts. To get the better acceleration and climbing ability with the wide ratio gears, that might not be too bad a trade. But the gear shifts with both stock gears and the wide ratio transmission do move engine speed to the limits of 10% of maximum torque.

For RVers who are satisfied with their present gearing for cruising but need additional accelerating and climbing power, the replacement gear set from Kilgore may be just what the doctor ordered. Cost of the gear set at the time of writing is $649.95. Installation can be done by any competent transmission mechanic. After getting the information from Kilgore, you can check with your mechanic for estimated labor charges.

If your transmission has indicated its intention to take an extended vacation, Kilgore has rebuilt units containing the replacement gear set and several other heavy duty modifications that make it nearly bullet proof. His modified transmissions are unconditionally guaranteed for one year with "no exceptions." That guarantee is a bit unusual in today's warranty climate.

Chapter 11

Gear Ratios... And What They Mean

In spite of the fact that many people talk knowingly about gear ratios, it's obvious from my mail that gear ratios remain a deep mystery. Adding to the confusion is the common practice of referring to low numerical ratios as being high and high numerical ratios as being low. Let's see if I can eliminate some of the confusion.

Engines develop both torque and horsepower. Torque is simply a twisting force applied to something that turns. In the case of engines, the force is applied to the crankshaft when the fuel burns and pushes the pistons down. Torque usually increases rapidly with increasing engine speed until it reaches its maximum value. Then it begins to decrease even though engine speed continues to increase. In most of our RV engines, maximum torque is developed at about 2500 revolutions per minute (rpm). That engine speed is also the most economical speed. More horsepower is developed per pound of fuel burned at near maximum torque speed than at any other engine speed.

Like torque, horsepower also rises with increasing engine speed and then falls off. But a typical engine develops maximum horsepower at a much higher speed than maximum torque. Most RV engines develop maximum horsepower at 3800 to 4400 rpm. The horsepower curve is also much steeper than the torque curve.

Gears in the differential or "rear end" reduce engine speed to wheel speed. For example, cruising down the highway at 60 mph, a popular size tire may be turning only 732 rpm while the engine is turning 2700 rpm to develop the power needed at that speed. The ratio of engine speed to wheel speed is the gear ratio that we've been talking about. A ratio of 4.00:1 (commonly spoken of as a ratio of 4) means that the engine turns 4 revolutions while the wheel is turning only one revolution. The higher the number of the ratio the faster the engine runs for a given road speed.

The actual gear ratio is determined by the number of teeth on two gears -- the ring and pinion gears, in the rear end. Due to the constraints of gear sizes and machining processes, the actual ratios are usually numbers such as 3.25, 3.55, 3.73, 4.10 and 4.55. At a given engine speed, a ratio of 3.25-1 will give a higher road speed than will a ratio of 4.10. That's the reason it's called a high ratio. Really, what is meant is that it is a high-speed ratio.

With RVs, we are not so concerned with high speed as we are with having enough power to move a heavy load, accelerate somewhat faster than a snail and climb mountains. Of course, it might be possible to install a huge, powerful engine and climb mountains at high speed. There are several problems with that approach. One is that huge, powerful engines are thirsty rascals even at low speeds. They are also heavy, inflict tremendous stresses on all parts of the drive system and are more expensive than you would believe. They also don't exist in factory vehicles. We are left with using the engines available from the factories and using gears that let the engines do the best job they can.

Another way of looking at gear ratios is in terms of levers. We all know that exerting a 50-pound force on a 6-foot lever will have greater effect than it will on a 3-foot lever. Higher numerical ratios let the engine work with a longer lever.

So, what gear ratio should we use? Theoretically, the best ratio would let the engine run at its maximum torque speed at the vehicle cruising speed we have selected. With most RV engines, that would be about 2500 rpm. That would be fine if the engine develops enough horsepower to maintain cruising speed and if we were content to stay at that speed and never accelerate to pass or never need to climb a hill. Since none of those "ifs" is a part of real life, we have to gear for a higher engine speed.

Let's look at an example. My favorite gasoline RV engine, the Ford 460, develops its maximum torque at 2200 rpm. Theoretically, that would be the best engine speed to gear for because at that engine speed it uses fuel most efficiently. But the engine can develop no more than 160 horsepower at that speed, even with wide-open throttle.

Suppose that our RV needs 160 horsepower to travel on a level road at 60 mph. With that gearing, there is no reserve engine power for passing or climbing. No one would be satisfied with the performance even though fuel economy might be relatively good.

That same engine can develop nearly 200 horsepower at 3000 rpm at wide-open throttle. But it can also develop the 160 horsepower required for 60 mph cruising at part throttle at 3000 rpm. That gives easy cruising and reserve horsepower for passing and climbing.

The correct gear ratio depends on many factors such as engine size, gross vehicle weight, tire size, terrain, and level of acceptable performance. Change any one of those factors, and you have changed the required gear ratio.

Let me give another example. My previous tow vehicle was a Ford van with 460 engine and 3.55 gears. It handled my 24-foot trailer very well, even in the Rocky mountains. There was always ample power and reasonable fuel economy. Then, I bought a used Ford Supercab with 351 engine and 3.55 gears. The weights of the two vehicles were nearly the same. The only thing changed was the engine size.

The morning I test-drove the truck and trailer for the first time, it was immediately obvious that performance was down. There was adequate power for travel in the Midwest, but I knew that traveling in my beloved Rockies was going to require some modifications. Besides some minor engine work, a gear change to 4.10 was indicated. If I had been certain that I would not travel outside the Midwest, I could have left things alone. But I knew that I would be "out West" that summer.

Why didn't I get the right gears when I bought the truck? When you buy used trucks, you don't get many choices. Whoever said there is virtue in being poor never tried it.

Another RVer I know quite well had an International Travelall that was an excellent tow vehicle for his trailer. On a trip to the Tetons, he developed several tire problems. He decided to replace all four tires with a set of 7.50-15s instead of the smaller H70-15s he had been using. Performance with the new tires was so bad that he subsequently found himself backing truck and trailer 1 1/2 miles down a mountain. The lesson? Tire size does affect gear ratio.

Recently, truck manufacturers have switched from 235/75-15 to 235/85-16 tires on their 3/4 ton trucks. Many owners have been disappointed with the performance of their new trucks with the same gear ratios as their older ones. The reason is not less engine power, but larger tires. The new tires require one step higher numerical gear ratio to maintain the same engine speed.

It's impossible to give a gear ratio or engine speed that will work with all RVers, but I will give some broad suggestions. With moderate loads and the largest engines available, most RVers will be satisfied with gearing for an engine speed of 2500 rpm at 55 mph. The same loads with 5.7-liter class engines will need engine speeds of around 2700-2800 rpm. Heavier loads with large engines will need to increase the engine speed to 2700-2800 rpm. With the largest trailers and heavy motorhomes, engine speed will need to be increased to 3000 rpm or more.

Many trailerists will say, "Yes, I can see that I need 4.10 gears for good towing performance, but, man, the solo fuel mileage will go to hell. Can't I get by with 3.55 gears and get better fuel mileage?"

You may get slightly better solo mileage, but towing mileage will likely be reduced. Towing performance will be degraded. And let me ask you this: If you had been in my brother's place as he was backing down that mountain with the tires sliding on the loose gravel and his family frightened to tears, how important would the extra 1 or 2 mpg in solo driving be?

Farlow's First Rule: The horsepower you don't buy will be the amount required to get over that next mountain. Power and gear for the tow and let the solo driving take care of itself.

For those of you who wisely buy those ideas but who still want to do something about solo mileage, the best answer is to install an auxiliary transmission such as the units from Gear Vendors or Doug Nash. Either of these lets you have the best of towing and solo performance. The new heavy-duty automatic overdrive transmissions such as Ford's E4OD do, too.

To give you some help in determining the proper ratio for your rig, here is an equation. Determine the diameter of your tires, your desired cruising speed, and the engine speed you want at that speed. Gear ratio = (rpm X tire diameter) / (mph X 336). If the answer you get is about half-way between available ratios, play it safe and go for the higher number ratio.

Chapter 12

Gear Vendors Overdrive Evaluation

Readers of my magazine columns know by now that I am a firm believer in aftermarket overdrive units. I prefer to call them auxiliary transmissions because that's what they are. All of them (except for one heavy-duty unit that is designed for heavier trucks) have two speeds, one higher than the other. If the output speed is faster than the input speed, it is called an overdrive. If the output speed is slower than the input, it is called an underdrive. Let's just call it a two-speed auxiliary transmission.

For several years, I used a Doug Nash auxiliary transmission. It gave excellent service with no problems from the day it was installed. My only objection to the Doug Nash was that the shift tended to be a bit harsher than I liked. To be honest, the jolt was no problem once I got used to it.

But I wanted to try the Gear Vendors unit for a variety of reasons. It uses a planetary gear set rather than the straight-cut gears found in other units. Planetary gears are quieter in operation. And shifting the Gear Vendors unit was reported by other writers to be so smooth as not to be noticed.

The cost of the Gear Vendors unit is the only drawback. It costs nearly twice as much as the Doug Nash, but it is rated for 30,000 pounds, which is a considerably higher rating. I didn't approach that kind of load, but it is always comforting to know that there is a high margin of capacity. Sale of my old van and purchase of a newer truck gave the excuse to test the Gear Vendors unit.

DO-IT-YOURSELF INSTALLATION

I like to install most of the equipment I test. It is important to me to be able to tell readers that a device can or cannot be installed by the average owner who has moderate mechanical abilities. That is also a test of the installation instructions. Some instructions I've seen are so confusing and poorly written that following them is more difficult than most owners would find comfortable. The instructions from Gear Vendors are very complete and clear. When I installed my unit, there was only one small glitch in the wiring instructions. At one place, the written instructions were incorrect. Fortunately, it was impossible to make the connection as written. A look at the wiring diagrams quickly straightened everything out.

Like most home mechanics, I don't have a hoist in my garage. To raise the rear of the truck I used a pair of ramps. Installation then meant that I was crawling under the truck and working in less than ideal conditions. (For one thing, temperatures were around 40 degrees.) In spite of all that, the tailshaft of my transmission was removed and the Gear Vendors unit installed in about three hours. You might be able to do it faster. No special tools were required, just a hydraulic jack to lift the transmission slightly and a handful of wrenches. Completing the wiring took another 45 minutes or so.

Installing the new driveshaft was a different matter. The instructions for measuring driveshaft angles were more complete than any I have seen anywhere else. Gear Vendors is to be congratulated for an excellent job. The problems I had were due to my own stupidity and the distance from a driveshaft shop.

My truck used a two-piece driveshaft. I wanted to preserve as much of the old shaft as possible so that when this truck is traded I could remove the Gear Vendors unit and return the truck to stock condition as easily as possible. My first intention was to replace the front portion of the driveshaft with a new front section.

FINE-TUNING THE DRIVESHAFT

I was not able to find a shop in the area that would balance a two-piece shaft. The next option was to get a new one-piece shaft made. It was a few inches longer than standard engineering specifications for a one-piece shaft, but the shop manager promised that he would have no trouble getting it to be vibration-free. Three trips later, the shaft still had a moderate but unacceptable vibration at cruising speed. My friendly mechanic and I used an old do-it-yourselfer's trick: We put it up on his hoist and used large hose clamps on the shaft to fine tune the balance. Trial and error completed the job in a few minutes.

How does the Gear Vendors unit work? Great. It is not a full-time unit like some others. That is, it always starts out in low range and does not shift into high range until it reaches either 20 mph or 40 mph. You select the speed on a dash-mounted switch. Turning the unit on or off is done by pressing a floor-mounted switch similar to a headlight dimmer switch. I located mine near where my left foot normally rests when driving. In operation, you may leave the unit turned on and let it shift automatically when it reaches the pre-selected shift speed or you may elect to make the shift using the floor switch.

A nice feature of the Gear Vendors unit is that it can be shifted under load. That is, you don't have to let up on the accelerator or shift the main transmission into neutral to shift between the two speeds. Just press the floor button, and the shift will be made. There is a slight jolt when shifting into high range under load, but it is not annoying. If you like, you can let up on the accelerator slightly when making the upshift and there is no jolt at all.

Shifting down is hardly noticeable, even under load.

FUEL SAVINGS: 20-30%

Gear Vendors advertises a 30% improvement in fuel mileage. I suppose that is possible in some instances, but I think most owners will get about 20%, as I did. A 20% savings in fuel will take a long time to pay the roughly $2,000 the unit costs. However, I think improved fuel mileage is one of the least important reasons for buying an auxiliary transmission. I bought mine for the improved performance it gives my tow vehicle.

I believe that a tow vehicle should be geared for towing; the rear end gears should be selected to let the engine run at a speed necessary to develop its power efficiently. In most instances, that means an engine speed of 2600 to 3000 rpm at a towing speed of 55 mph. Thus, the engine runs faster than necessary when running solo at the higher solo cruising speeds. Far less power is needed, and the engine can run slower and be more efficient. The addition of an auxiliary transmission with an overdrive output gives me that. My truck has a rear end ratio of 4.11-1. With the Gear Vendors unit, I have an overall solo cruising ratio of 3.20. That gives me the best of both worlds and is one reason I like an auxiliary transmission.

The other reason is the extra gears I have for towing. I spend a lot of time towing in the Rockies. With the Gear Vendors unit, I have five towing speeds. I can start up the mountain in third on the main transmission and low range on the Gear Vendors. When engine speed drops to about 2400 rpm, I shift to second and high. That moves the engine speed back to its best pulling speed. As engine speed again drops to 2400, I shift to second and low and regain engine speed. The process continues until we get to the top of the mountain. On the way down the other side, I have all of those combinations again to give the best combination of engine braking and road speed.

Put those two reasons together with a 20% improvement in fuel mileage, and an auxiliary transmission makes a lot of sense.

Is the Gear Vendors unit worth its cost? I think so. It should last at least as long as the main transmission. With the choice of adapters available, I should have no trouble installing it on my next truck and the one after that. Somewhere down the line, it may need to be overhauled. No problem. Somewhere down the line, I may need an overhaul, too.

I would like to see truck manufacturers make two-speed rear ends available in their light trucks. Until they do, auxiliary transmissions give the same effect. With their easy interchangeability from one truck to another, they may even be better.

The Gear Vendors unit is excellent. Quality of construction is superb. Installation instructions are very complete and easy to follow. And installation is as easy as any such installation can be.

Chapter 13

Hitched, hitched: Let's Get Hitched

There's nothing very amusing about anyone towing a trailer that isn't on the level, but I find it funny. Funny as in strange. Why would anyone deliberately give himself added trouble and discomfort? I don't know why, but they do. All you have to do is look at trailers and tow vehicles as they go by or when they are parked at rest stops. There they sit, with the rear of the tow vehicle down and the rear of the trailer up. Or sometimes it's the other way around.

I enjoy towing a trailer, but some people don't. For many, it's their own fault. They don't get hitched up right. A trailer that doesn't ride on the level is miserable to pull. Every bump, every change in speed exerts a force on the tow vehicle that causes it to bob or rock up and down. That's not very comfortable for the people riding in the tow vehicle. That unnecessary motion also imposes extra wear on the suspension systems of both the tow vehicle and the trailer. And everything inside the trailer tries to migrate to the front or the rear. Let's change all that. Let's get hitched right.

You'll need a tape measure, a large adjustable wrench and a pipe wrench. Drive to a large, paved area that is as nearly flat as possible. A mall parking lot is usually good. Select a spot out of the way and drive straight ahead for about 50 feet to get the trailer and tow vehicle in a straight line. Unhook the tow vehicle and move it ahead a couple of inches. Carefully level the trailer to the pavement. Measure the distance from points on the trailer frame in the front and rear to the pavement and adjust the trailer until they are the same. Make a note of the measurements.

THE RIGHT BALL HEIGHT

Now measure the distance from the pavement to the top, inside of the ball socket on the trailer. Measure the distance from the pavement to the top of the ball. The ball should be about a half inch to three-fourths inch higher than the top of the socket. If it isn't, either raise or lower the ball mount to get it the right height if you have an adjustable ball mount.

If the ball mount is not adjustable and the ball is too low, buy a ball with a longer shank to get the height you need. If the ball mount is not adjustable and the present ball is too high, you may have to go back to the hitch shop and have them cut the ball mount loose and weld it to the proper height. That's a nuisance, but driving with the hitch improperly adjusted is worse.

Now that you have the ball height properly set, carefully measure on the tow vehicle from the pavement to some easily identified spot on the front and rear bumper. Note these measurements. Now hitch up. The back of the tow vehicle will sag. Use tension on the equalizing bars to bring the back of the tow vehicle up to where it looks about right. Measure the heights of the front and rear of the tow vehicle again. Both should be lower than before. The ideal adjustment will have both ends of the tow vehicle drop the same distance. Adjust the tension on the bars until you get as close to that ideal as you can.

THE CORRECT CHAIN LINKS

While you're at it, check to see that the chains from the ends of the equalizing bars are perpendicular to the bars. You may need to move the brackets on the trailer frame a bit to get the chains perpendicular. One way to be sure you can repeat the bar tension the next time you hook up is to mark the chain link that is on the hook or in the slot. I simply tie a short piece of wire through that link.

If you're using Reese cam-type sway bars, be sure the cam arms are adjusted so that they ride the bars correctly. The deep pocket of the bars should be centered on the cam on the arms. If you're using a friction type sway bar, follow the manufacturer's instructions for adjustment. If you don't have the instructions, you can usually safely set the portion on the trailer frame so that about half the sliding portion is exposed when the two vehicles are in a straight line. Adjust the tension to eliminate sway.

Adjusting the PullRite hitch is slightly different. PullRite instructions call for initial placement of the ball about an inch below the top of the ball socket instead of above it. Setting initial tension on the bars is similar. When driving with the PullRite hitch, if you hear a knocking from the hitch on slight bumps, tighten the bars one at a time until the knocking is eliminated. Another difference between the two types of hitches is that you won't use any sway bars with the PullRite hitch.

That should get you hitched right. If your water tanks are in the front of your trailer and were empty, you will probably need to tighten the bars a notch when the tanks are full. Likewise, if you decide to carry an unusually heavy load in the back of the tow vehicle, you may have to add a bit of tension. The idea is to distribute the loads so that both vehicles are level.

Chapter 14

Hoses, Cords and Adapters

For some reason, hoses are on my mind. Maybe it's because for the first time in 30 years of RVing I came up short. My sewer hose was short, that is. I tugged and pulled and tried every way to get an extra three feet out of the hose, but all that I accomplished was to pull the hose loose from its connector. Oh, well.

Fortunately, I was camping for the weekend with my brother, and he happened to have an extra piece of hose and a coupler. Mighty embarrassing for big brother to have to borrow from little brother. You can be sure I'll have enough hose next time.

Sewer hoses are one of those items we tend not to think about until we need them. I knew that sooner or later I would find a spot where the park designer hadn't located the sewer drain to fit my trailer. But, like a lot of other RVers, I didn't think about hoses between trips.

One solution to having enough sewer hose is to buy one of those 20-foot lengths and always use that. Twenty feet will reach even the most poorly located sewer connector. It also makes an unsightly mess when the sewer is only five feet away. And if you've got a small dog, it can get lost in the coils and not found until time to leave the park.

TWO LENGTHS OF HOSE

The answer is to have two lengths of sewer hose. Most of the time a section about six feet long is enough. Get another section 10 feet long, and the two coupled together will reach almost any sewer. Or buy a 20-foot hose if you need a new one and cut it into two pieces.

Of course, with two lengths of hose, you need a coupler. You can opt for the low-cost model that requires hose clamps. But the hose clamps require a screw driver to make sure you get the clamp tight enough. It's embarrassing to think you've got the clamp tight enough and find out you were wrong. And where is the screw driver when you need it, Charlie? (That's grist for a chapter in my next book.)

A better connector is one that has large, deep screw threads as part of the connector. Just turn the connector into the hose by hand and it's securely fastened. No normal handling will pull the hoses apart.

While you're at it, buy a 90-degree sewer adapter for the park end of the hose. It looks more professional -- well, aren't you a professional camper? -- and it seals the sewer connection against unappetizing odors. Both connectors are available from well-equipped RV dealers or from Camping World.

TIE A STRING AROUND IT

Have you ever lost your sewer hose? How does one lose a sewer hose? Well, one way is to put it in the hose bumper and drive 50 miles. While you're driving, the hose gets antsy and crawls to the other end of the bumper. Then you have to find something to pull it out. Outwit that antsy hose by tying a piece of heavy string around the outer end just behind the connector. Leave about six inches of string dangling. Stuff the hose into the bumper with the string hanging out. Close the bumper door and the string is caught. The hose can't crawl away, and you don't have to look for something to coax it out. Saves a lot of cussing, too.

On the subject of sewer hoses, always use yours when you dump the holding tank. From the looks of many dump stations, there are a lot of RVers who take a short cut and just dump, hoping that the contents will make it. Then they don't bother to use the rinse hose to clean up. They're the same ones that complain first when dumping stations get closed. Let's all keep it clean. Cleaning takes only a couple of minutes longer.

There's another hose that we all use, too. That's the water hose. How do you store yours? I've seen some of your hoses. It's a wonder any water ever finds it way through all those kinks and turns. The answer, again, is two hoses plus a couple of small reels. One short hose about 10 feet long will usually connect you to the park water supply. Why drag around a 50-foot hose when 10 feet are enough. Then carry a second section 25 feet or so for those tough spots. Buy or make a reel to hold each piece of hose. That eliminates the hose tangles, makes the hoses last longer, and they take up less storage space.

When you store the hoses, connect the two ends together unless you like the idea of spiders and other critters in your drinking water.

A lot of parks have very high water pressure. Your hoses and your RV's plumbing were never intended for such high pressures. Connecting to one of those water systems may help you find the weak spot in your plumbing. Some park operators will tell you their water system operates at 120 pounds of pressure. Others believe in letting you find out for yourself. Buy an inexpensive pressure regulator and leave it attached to the hose you use most often.

WHERE'S THAT HOSE BEEN?

You say you never connect to the park system? You just fill your tank from the hose the park left there for you? If you saw where that hose has been you would never drink water again. Some hoses frequent some pretty rotten places. Get your own and use it. I always add half an ounce of household bleach to a 30-gallon water tank when I refill. The clean hose and bleach help us to avoid having to do the amoebic quickstep. I never could dance, anyway.

So much for hoses. Now for cords, the extension variety. Too often the cord that comes with the RV reaches to within three feet of the outlet box. Why is it park developers love to put the outlet box in the back 40? It's time for the cord stretcher. What, no cord stretcher? Okay, dig in the kit for the extension cord. No, that rat's nest can't be your extension cord. It is? Well, Charlie, you're in trouble. By the time you get all the tangles out, it will be Sunday evening. Anyway, that cord isn't heavy enough to carry the load.

When electric current runs through a wire, it meets resistance. The resistance produces heat and less electrical current. Heat produces fire. It's that simple. Your RV needs a cord heavy enough carry the required electric current without developing heat. If you don't have an air conditioner or an electric heater, you can probably get by with a 15-amp 10/3 heavy-duty cord. One air conditioner or electric heater calls for a 30-amp 10/3 heavy-duty cord.

More than one air conditioner puts you in the 50-amp area for good electrical performance.

MULTIPLE SHORT CORDS

I suggest that instead of a 100-foot cord, you get two 25-foot cords and, perhaps, one 50-foot in the right size for your power needs. That way you don't have to handle so much cord when only a short extension is needed. Put them on their own reels. You can buy plastic reels or make your own out of scraps of plywood.

So now you're organized, at least as far as hoses and cords go. Oh, one thing more. The next time somebody gets the shock of his life, literally, when he climbs into his RV won't be the first time. The problem is that too many park outlets are wired wrong so that current is carried on the wrong wire. The result can well be that the skin of your RV, which is not supposed to carry any electrical current, can be hotter than a $2 pistol in a Texas jail break. Touch the RV skin while standing on the ground and your ears and eyes will light up brightly, but not for very long.

How to avoid this situation that can ruin your plans permanently? Buy a ground monitor and use it every time you hook up to an outlet box. It's a simple, little gadget that you plug into an outlet. Illuminated signals let you know whether the outlet has been wired correctly. But having the monitor won't do a bit of good if you don't use it -- every time you hook up. With the knowledge that the outlet is wired correctly you can hook up safely. Then when you touch your RV and stand on the ground at the same time, you may not create quite as much sensation, but you'll live longer.

Chapter 15

Level Parking On Unlevel Ground

One thing I quickly discovered when I first began RVing was that campsites are often not level. In fact, only recently has there been much interest by campground developers in furnishing fairly level sites. Many older campgrounds still have campsites that have only minimal attention to a level parking pad.

The result is, well, interesting. Walk around any older campground in hilly terrain, and you are likely to find RVs parked in such a way as to make life inside a bit disturbing. Trying to fry an egg becomes an exercise in keeping the egg in the skillet. Juice slips out the other side of the glass. Staying in bed becomes a gymnastic event. Moving from one end of the rig to the other gets you ready for climbing hills.

And the poor refrigerator dies.

A refrigerator repairman once told me that you can ruin a refrigerator in an hour by parking off level. Some of the new models are more tolerant of an unlevel condition that the older ones, but all will cool more efficiently and last longer if the rig is parked level. When parking on the level is so easy and the living so much more comfortable, why tolerate an unlevel condition?

FIRST THE LEVELING BLOCKS

There are a couple of things you'll need. One is a simple set of leveling blocks. The other is a level. Nearly any level will do, but there is one type that makes the job so much easier that I wouldn't want to be without it. The one I have mounts on the front of the trailer where it can be seen from the driver's seat. It indicates both side-to-side level and lengthwise level conditions. Motorhome owners could mount it on the dash panel.

Before mounting the level, park your rig on a level surface. The usual instructions say to place a small level on the freezer coils. In most installations, that's a bit absurd; the level can't be read in that position.

It's easier and sufficiently accurate to get the bottom of the refrigerator level. You may have to drive up on a couple of boards. Use the jackpost on a trailer to level lengthwise. When you've got the rig as level as you can, mount the level where you can see it from the driver's seat and be sure it indicates a level condition from side to side. Mount it on a surface that is as vertical as possible. You may need to use some thin shims to get the level vertical.

ADJUSTING THE BUBBLE

On most levels of this type there are two tubes. The large one is for the side-to-side condition. The small one is for lengthwise and has an adjusting screw. After the level is mounted, adjust the screw to center the lengthwise bubble.

That's the hard part, but it needs to be done only once. All you have to do now to level your rig in a site is slowly back into the site until both tubes indicate your rig is level. That will rarely happen, so position your rig where you want it and take a look at the levels. The large tube is marked in segments. On mine, each segment indicates the need for a piece of 2 X 4 lumber to raise that side to level. You will quickly learn what the markings mean for your rig.

After you've determined how much correction is needed, pull forward, place the correct amount of blocks in place, and while watching the level, back into place. Stop when the bubble centers. Unhook your trailer and use the jack post to level lengthwise while watching the other bubble. Motorhome owners without a power leveling system will have to try a couple of times to get all four wheels properly positioned.

MAKING LEVELING BLOCKS

To make the use of leveling blocks easier, cut lengths of 2 X 6 lumber. You need four pieces, 60 inches, 54 inches, 48 inches and 42 inches long. I cut an angle on one end of each piece. Just stack them to get the amount needed for your site. Motorhome owners may need two sets, but they can be shorter for single axles. I drilled three-eighths-inch holes through the stack so I could loosely insert a couple of 60 penny spikes to hold the stack from slipping, but I haven't found it necessary to use them.

Until now I've carried a six-inch block of wood about five inches thick to use under the jack post. That sometimes is too short or too thick. So, I'm making an adjustable block. Get a piece of pipe that will slip inside the jack post. Get as long a piece as you can insert when the jack is fully retracted. Mount it to a floor flange. (A floor flange is a piece of cast iron threaded to accept the pipe thread and has a flat surface with four holes for screws. Buy it at the same place you buy the pipe.) Mount the flange to a piece of three-fourths-inch plywood about six inches square. Drill holes through both sides of the pipe about two inches apart starting about an inch above the floor flange. Get a long bolt or piece of rod to fit through the holes.

In use. slip the pipe inside the jack post. Slip the iron rod through the holes in the pipe that will give you the height you need. Simple. No more stacking blocks that might slip in the night. I hate things that go bump in the night.

Chapter 16

Luxurious Luxury

What do you get when you spend $200,000 or more for a motorhome? Fair question. With dozens of motorhomes selling for a fraction of that amount, what does spending from $200,000 to over $450,000 buy?

The editors of "COAST TO COAST" magazine asked me to check it out. One thing I found immediately is that you don't walk into your neighborhood RV dealer to look at the top models. Few dealers could afford to stock a $300,000 motorhome. I'm sure that there are dealers somewhere who are ready to show motorhomes with names like Foretravel, Country Coach, Monaco, Newell and Bluebird, to name a few, but those dealers haven't set up shop in Milwaukee.

If you want to see the luxury models "up close and personal," the easiest way is to attend one of the big RV shows. Wear something that gives the impression you could pay the price, leave the kids at home and prepare to drool. Luxury models of motorhomes exude quality and a style of travel that speak for themselves. Solid oak or walnut cabinetry is the norm. There is none of the thin veneer or paneling with imitation wood grain found on lesser models. Expensive fabrics and leather upholstery are also prominent. Rugs and carpets look and feel as if they escaped from the Presidential Suite of an expensive hotel or an oil baron's mansion. Padded ceilings with acoustical headliners are common. Soft, deep cushions on all seats

and couches invite terminal relaxation. Who would want to climb out of such luxury and do something so mundane as go for a hike?

Appliances also are designed to invite the mind to soar. Built-in vacuum cleaners are standard. Many models have multiple built-in TV sets with VCRs. No self-respecting luxury motorhome manufacturer would expect you to have to add a microwave oven. Trash compactors are found in nearly all models. Icemakers and separate freezers are commonplace. Central air conditioning is a given. Hydronic heat for quiet, even heating is standard on some models. Owners of luxury coaches are not expected to stumble around in the night, so built-in floor-level night lights are supplied. And the list goes on.

THERE'S MORE SPACE, TOO!

Space is one item frequently listed as standard in luxury motorhomes. Much of the space comes from the length, of course. Expensive motorhomes run from 34 to 40 feet long. Additional space comes from a recent federal ruling permitting certain classes of vehicles to exceed the 96-inch width restriction. Motorhomes fall into the

exempted class. Most luxury coaches are 102 inches wide. The extra six inches may not seem like much, but in a 40-foot coach, it gives an extra 20 square feet of space.

Owners of motorhomes in the $200,000 and up class are likely to carry valuables such as jewelry with them. The question arises as to how safe a motorhome might be for storage of expensive items. Most luxury model coaches solve the problem by including a hidden safe as either a standard or optional item.

Other conveniences include large built-in generators, telephone wiring and external connections, heavy-duty inverters and multiple storage batteries to supply 110-volt AC current when there is no shoreline connection. Thick foam insulation keeps the inside temperatures at a comfortable level. Large fuel tanks holding as much as 200 gallons of fuel give long-range cruising. Large fresh water tanks mean less worrying about running out of water in the middle of a shower. Propane tanks can contain as much as 270 gallons. Built-in closed-circuit television lets the driver know what's behind the coach. Built-in computerized leveling systems take the guesswork and crawling out of parking and leveling. Huge basement-style storage units make it easy to decide what goes and what stays. Everything can go.

NO TUBS ALLOWED?

Some few luxury coaches contain large tubs in the

bathroom -- one or two manufacturers even venture to call their tubs spas, but I was surprised to find that most dispense with a bathtub. Large showers are most common. Many models don't even offer a tub option.

Up front, the control room resembles nothing so much as the cockpit of a jumbo jetliner. Gauges give readouts on 30 or more engine and travel conditions from engine temperature to water pressure to exhaust temperature to things you never even thought about before. The pilot and co-pilot chairs are straight from a driver's dreams. Power adjustments and foam and leather upholstery assure that no part of your body will feel discomfort. Electrically heated outside mirrors will never be obscured by ice or snow. Power steering, air brakes and cruise control guarantee effortless long-distance travel.

Mechanically, luxury coaches continue the, well, luxury. Engines have names like Caterpillar, Detroit Diesel and Cummins, all diesels. Most engines are turbocharged for even more powerful performance. Heavy-duty engine heaters for easy cold morning starts are usually standard. Allison transmissions are the norm. Most include Jake brakes as standard or an option to eliminate the white knuckles from descending mountain grades. Air ride or other luxury suspension systems take all the bumps out of travel. Of course, luxury coaches are heavy and require brakes comparable to their weight. No problem. Air brakes are universal. Most coaches have Michelin radial tires as standard equipment.

PAYLOAD AND FUEL ECONOMY

Important but sometimes overlooked, the chassis have ample weight ratings to carry all the luxuries. Payloads, the difference between empty weight and maximum allowable weight, of 10,000 pounds are not unusual. Some have even more payload.

It would seem that moving all of that weight -- 30,000 pounds or more -- down the road would result in fuel mileage figures that give headaches and snail-like acceleration. Not so. Many owners of luxury coaches report 8 to 12 miles per gallon. But you get the feeling that the owners don't really care. Performance is something that we can all talk about without seeming crass, though. Because the huge engines in luxury motorhomes have high horsepower and torque figures, acceleration and hill-climbing are often much better than on lighter weight models.

Handling will probably never equal that of a taut sports car, but one test driver was moved to describe the test motorhome as deserving "rave reviews as a handling machine, even from die-hard automobile aficionados." Surprisingly, some owners of luxury models don't care how they handle. Several years ago I read of such an owner who was asked about the handling characteristics of his $400,000 plus coach. "To tell the truth," he said, "I don't know. I've never driven it. My chauffeur does all the driving." No, before you ask, chauffeurs are not part of the standard equipment.

There's one more thing that comes with a luxury motorhome -- prestige. It's not an option. Prestige comes standard. Anyone looking at a coach by Foretravel or Beaver or Newell or any of the other top lines immediately recognizes that a lot of money went into the coach. Perhaps driving a $300,000 coach won't get you through the service station any faster or get you a better parking spot at a camping resort. But certainly it will get you a lot of envious looks. That's worth something, and you get a lot of it for $200,000 or more.

Just walking through a $200,000 motorhome is enough to cause the most devout Puritan to lust after riches. Whether or not you presently aspire to owning such an expensive coach, you owe it to yourself to look a couple over at the next big RV show. You may find an expensive, new goal in life. It wouldn't be the worst possible goal to strive for.

Who Builds Them?

The following is a list of those manufacturers I could find who build motorhomes costing over $200,000. There may be others.

Barth Motor Company
P.O. Box 768
Milford, IN 46542

Beaver Coaches, Inc.
P.O. Box 6089
Bend, OR 97708

Blue Bird Wanderlodge
One Wanderlodge Way
Fort Valley, GA 31030

Country Coach, Inc.
135 East First Street
Junction City, OR 97448

Foretravel, Inc.
1221 N.W. Stallings Drive
Nacogdoches, TX 75961

Monaco Coach Corporation
325 East First Street
Junction City, OR 97448

Newell Coach Corporation
P.O. Box 1185
Miami, OK 74335

Chapter 17

Manuals: Data For Doing It Right

The water pump on your motorhome is in the process of mugging itself, and you hate having to pay a mechanic to replace it when you believe you can do it yourself. But you're not sure where to start. You know you could replace the ignition module yourself -- if you just had a little information. Replacing the shocks should be an easy do-it-yourself job, but which end should be removed first, or does it make any difference?

RVers are great at getting their hands dirty digging into the works of their rigs. Doing your own maintenance and at least light repairs makes sense in saving money. It also makes sense in being more familiar with your rig. Even if you aren't going to do the work yourself, you can save money and steer clear of unnecessary repairs if you know what goes on mechanically with your RV. And often you can find a problem while it is still small and inexpensive if you know what to look for. Having the right information can also help you decide which jobs are beyond your ability. That can save you money, too.

A continuing problem for RVers is locating information needed to make those repairs or do that maintenance. Well, good news! The information is easily available. There is a wealth of repair manuals available, and they don't cost more than the repair. Some of them you can get from the company that built the chassis of your motorhome. Some of them you can buy at your nearest bookstore. Many of them are available at your

local library. Stay with me for a few minutes, and together we'll take a look at what's available and where you can get it.

Getting information for do-it-yourself maintenance and repair on motorhomes is complicated by the way motorhomes are manufactured. In most instances, the motorhome manufacturer doesn't build chassis. It buys them from a truck manufacturer or a specialty chassis builder. Then it assembles the motorhome body to the chassis. In some instances it may use more than one make of chassis for the same model motorhome. Ask the motorhome manufacturer for a service manual, and you'll be told there isn't one and there isn't money to hire someone to write such a manual.

FACTORY VS. INDEPENDENT MANUALS

Are you out of luck? Usually not. Fortunately, the company that made the chassis also had some manuals written. Too, there are some independent companies that publish manuals for the most popular model chassis. Which is better, the company manual or the one from an independent? That's not so easy to answer. It depends on you, your mechanical ability and what you want to do.

Factory manuals are written for the mechanics in

local dealer repair facilities. A high level of expertise and experience is assumed. That doesn't mean that you wouldn't find them useful, however. One big problem with factory manuals is that they are written in the year the chassis is built. As the chassis is used by thousands of buyers, problems arise and solutions are found. The solutions find their way back to the dealers through service bulletins. Unless you subscribe to the service bulletins, you'll never get that new information.

Independent publishers approach manuals a bit differently. Their manuals are designed to cover a span of several years and are updated annually. As chassis modifications are made and new service procedures established, the changes appear in new editions of the manuals. That can be a real help for most of us.

TYPES OF MANUALS

Independent manuals fall into at least two general classes. One group, exemplified by Chilton's popular series, deals with a particular make and model. For example, Chilton has a volume for Ford vans covering all years from 1961 to 1988. While not specifically for Class C motorhomes, this volume would be useful for motorhomes built on the Ford van chassis for those years. There are similar volumes for Dodge and Chevrolet vans. The volumes for Datsun and Toyota pickups would be useful for owners of micro-minis built on these chassis.

This series of manuals has very complete step by step instructions for repairs and tuneups of all systems and components. Also included are complete specifications and capacities for the models covered. In addition to repair and tuneup instructions, there are sections of general interest such as ways to improve economy and suggestions on purchasing tools. Only a moderate level of expertise is assumed. Most owners of Class C motorhomes would find these manuals very useful. They are available in most book stores for less than $13.

The other type of independently published manual covers a class of vehicle or chassis for all manufacturers during a span of several years. The best known are "Chilton's Truck and Van Repair Manual" and "Motor Truck Repair Manual." Chilton's manual covers all makes of light trucks through one ton capacity. The Motor manual covers all trucks and vans from the lightest to the heaviest. Both are updated annually. Both have highly detailed specifications and clear step-by-step instructions for replacement and adjustment of components. Most operations are illustrated with very clear drawings. Neither manual includes wiring diagrams.

The Chilton manual has separate sections on repairing mechanical components such as air conditioning, electrical systems, emissions systems, carburetors, steering, transmissions and differentials. The Chilton manual also has an excellent trouble-shooting and diagnosis section. Both manuals assume a fairly high degree of expertise but certainly not beyond that of a skillful amateur. They are available in most bookstores for less than $30. They can also be found in most libraries.

LOOK AT THE OPTIONS

I grew up with a Motor Manual and continue to find the new editions useful. Obviously, if your motorhome uses a chassis rated at more than one ton, the Chilton manual would not be for you. If you have a Class C rig, either would be useful.

If your motorhome is built on the popular Chevrolet P-series chassis, you might want to take a look at the "Light Duty Truck Service Manual" by Chevrolet. This volume covers pick-ups, vans and P-trucks. Illustrations are clear, as are maintenance schedules and service locations on the chassis. I found the instructions for replacement of components less detailed than either the Chilton or Motor manuals. There are good diagnosis suggestions for most systems and common problems. There is a section on servicing electrical components, but no wiring diagrams.

Wiring diagrams are contained in a separate volume, "Chevrolet 10-30 Series Light Duty Truck Wiring Diagrams." These manuals can be found in some libraries. You can also order them through your local Chevrolet dealer. There should be ordering information in your operator's manual -- if you've got one.

If your motorhome uses a Chevrolet chassis, there are two other publications you'll want, and the prices are right. They are free. Write to Chevrolet Motor Division, 30007 Van Dyke, Room 136-130, Warren, Michigan 48090 and ask for "Recreational Vehicle Service Directory" and "Chevrolet Motorhome Chassis Service Guide." The directory is a list of more than 3,000 GM dealers around the country who will work on motorhomes. The guide is a synopsis of bulletins and maintenance information on problems that commonly occur with motorhomes built on the GM van and P-series chassis.

SEPARATE FORD MANUALS

Ford chooses to do things differently. Instead of one manual covering all systems, it has separate manuals.

For example, there is a manual on engine/emissions diagnosis that covers all truck models. While the manuals are very complete, you would have to buy several manuals to cover all the systems on your chassis. These can ordered either through your local Ford dealer or using the information in your operator's manual.

Factory manuals cost from $15 to $100, depending upon what is covered and the method of distribution.

Which manual is best for you? As I said earlier, that depends on you and what you want to do. I consider myself to be an above-average amateur. I have come to depend upon the Chilton series for one make and model. But I would always want to have the appropriate volume of Motor Manual available. If I owned a Class A motorhome, I would have to choose something else. If my motorhome used the Chevrolet P-series chassis, I would likely opt for the factory manual and have a Motor Manual handy.

If you look in dealer's repair shops, you'll find factory manuals, or course. If you look in independent garages, you'll find a few factory manuals and a lot of Chilton's and Motor Manuals. I strongly suggest you look at all of them before making your purchase.

OTHER MOTORHOME CHASSIS

What about those of you who have motorhomes built on John Deere, Gillig, Spartan, or one of the other specialty chassis? Your options are different. These chassis manufacturers use standard engines, transmissions, differentials and braking systems that are used on thousands of trucks. You can buy the appropriate factory manuals for your engine, transmission and differential. "Motor Truck Repair Manual" would cover most of the components used. Or you could try getting a service manual directly from the chassis manufacturer. You might even be successful.

Using service manuals can be very interesting and productive. If you do your own maintenance and light repair work, you can save lots of money that can be spent on more trips. Even if you don't own a wrench, you will still save money by learning more about what makes your RV run -- and sometimes quit. And who knows? Maybe you'll decide to buy a few wrenches and other tools and get a little grease on your hands.

Chapter 18

Power Tuning Your Engine

Would you like to find a way to get about 10 per cent better mileage at a cost of nothing but a couple of hours of your time? Yes, I'll bet you're thinking, I'd like to sell you some real estate with a bridge on it up in New York, too.

Well, someone beat you to the bridge. But I do have a way to power tune your engine that can give you up to 10 per cent better mileage and costs only time. Unless you have a Chevy or one of the new EFI engines. With a Chevy, you'll have to spend a few bucks, but not much. I don't have an answer for the EFI engines yet.

As I've said before, our vehicles come from the factory designed with lots of built-in compromises. The factory engineers have to make some assumptions about the way you drive without knowing anything about you. They also have to consider the governmental mandates on mileage and emissions. But one of the biggest variables they have to allow for is that no two engines are exactly alike. That's true even when they come off the same line.

In manufacturing any product, it is impossible to build to an absolute size. A cylinder, for example, may be designed to be 4.255 inches in diameter. But it is impossible to hold all cylinders to exactly that size. So they permit tolerances. Some cylinders will be slightly smaller and some slightly larger. The same thing is true of the piston that fits those cylinders.

THE FIT CAN BE SLOPPY

So what happens when one cylinder with maximum allowable size meets a piston with minimum allowable size? You're right: a relatively sloppy fit. Suppose that all eight cylinders in your engine happen to be that kind of fit? Now consider that the next engine down the line just happens to have the opposite set of tolerances. Which engine would you prefer?

Which engine did you get? I don't know either, and neither do the engineers. But they do know that somebody got both engines, and they both have to run reasonably well. So they prescribe a set of operating specifications that will work fairly well with all engines under a presumed set of operating conditions.

You can bet those conditions are not yours. You can also bet that your engine will run better if its operating specifications are fine-tuned for its set of tolerances.

Legally, your mechanic can't do it. That's especially true if you go to the dealer. By law, mechanics are supposed to use the set of specifications determined by the factory. The idea is to ensure that engine emissions meet the guidelines. Well, there is almost nothing on my engine that meets the specifications, but every January it beats the emissions requirements by a wide margin. And my fuel economy has improved from 13 mpg when I got the vehicle to 18 mpg with 125,000 miles on it.

Can you do it too? Maybe not all of it, but that 10 per cent I mentioned would not be bad.

HERE'S THE STARTING POINT

Where to start? The easiest place to get better mileage and more power is with ignition timing. On all gasoline engines, the timing is set for the spark to occur at some point just before the piston reaches top dead center on the compression stroke. The amount ahead of top dead center is called the advance. There are three types of advance that we have to work with.

Initial advance is the amount of advance in degrees that occurs when the engine is idling, before any other advance comes in. Initial advance has to be kept low so that the engine will idle well and start easily. As engine speed increases, more advance is needed because things are happening more rapidly in the cylinders. It takes time for the flame front of the burning gasoline to move across the cylinder. The time is roughly the same whether the engine is idling at 800 rpm or running at 4000 rpm.

To make sure the flame front has time to do its thing, the amount of advance increases with engine speed. That is called centrifugal or mechanical advance because it is controlled by a set of centrifugal weights in the distributor. As engine speed increases, the weights move out and deliver more ignition advance until the maximum designed advance occurs at somewhere over 3200 rpm.

When an engine is operating under a heavy load, the combustion pressures inside the cylinders increase. That causes the flame front to travel faster. It can also cause some of the fuel/oxygen mixture to self-ignite if the pressure gets too high. That's one of the causes of ping. But when you are cruising down the road with a light load, the combustion pressures are lower. What all that means is that an engine running at cruising speed under a light load can use even more ignition advance than one under a heavy load at the same speed.

ADJUSTING VACUUM ADVANCE

To accommodate those differences, engineers dial in the third kind of advance -- vacuum advance. It works because, under a light load, the manifold vacuum will be higher than under a heavy load. There is a diaphragm device on the side of the distributor that reads the amount of vacuum (engine load) and controls the vacuum advance. What most mechanics seem not to realize is that the vacuum advance can be adjusted. On Fords, the vacuum advance device from the factory is adjustable with an Allen wrench. The same is true of at least some Chrysler products. On GMs, you have to buy an adjustable vacuum advance from your local speed shop. The one I have used is made by Crane Cams.

So, let's do it. You'll need a wrench that fits the hold-down bolt on your distributor, a 3/32 Allen wrench and a golf tee. A timing light will help but isn't essential. Disconnect the hose from the vacuum advance and plug it with the golf tee. Find a stretch of road that doesn't have much traffic and note two markers about a tenth of a mile apart. If you have a Ford with automatic transmission, put it in second gear. With other automatics, just use drive. Line up with your first mark and floor the accelerator and hold it there. Note the speed as accurately as you can when you pass the second mark. Did you hear any ping? A lot or very slight?

Go back to your first mark and shut off the engine. If you heard no ping at all, you want to give a bit more initial advance. If you heard a lot of ping, you want to take some advance out. If the ping was very light, leave it alone.

To make adjustments, first determine the rotation of the inner workings of the distributor. The easy way is to make a fist with your right hand with your index finger extended. Place the bottom of your fist over the distributor with your index finger over the vacuum advance. If you can't, then use your left hand the same way. In either case, your index finger points the direction of rotation of the rotor. Loosen the hold-down clamp. Carefully turn the distributor for greater or lesser advance according to what you determined you need. How much? That's the question. If you have a timing light, try two degrees. Without a light, try about a quarter of an inch of distributor movement. Tighten the clamp. Run your test again.

THE FINAL STEPS

Assuming that you dialed in more advance, you're now looking for a slightly faster top speed at the second marker. If you still get no ping at all, go back to mark one and put in another two degrees of advance. Repeat the steps until you get ping. Then take out half of the last adjustment. If you have a timing light, check to see how much advance you now have and make note of it. You may find that engine speed has increased enough that you will need to adjust idle speed on the carburetor.

Now plug the vacuum line back onto the vacuum advance unit. Go for a ride at 30 mph. Listen carefully for ping. If there is any ping, stop and remove the vacuum hose from the distributor. Insert a 3/32 Allen wrench in the neck where the hose was connected. Turn clockwise two turns, reinstall hose and drive again at 30. If ping continues, repeat until you get rid of it. If there was no ping on first trial, accelerate to 50 mph. If there is any ping, repeat the steps mentioned above for adjusting.

If there is no ping, turn Allen wrench counter-clockwise two turns and drive again at 50 mph. Repeat until you get slight ping on acceleration at 50. Then adjust vacuum advance one turn clockwise. That should do it.

You may find that you get some ping when pulling a load. If so, just adjust the vacuum advance clockwise one turn at a time until you get rid of the ping. What you are doing is setting the load at which the vacuum advance retards timing to adjust for the load.

By following the steps outlined, you have tailored the ignition advance to your engine and the way you drive. You should get a noticeable increase in mileage and power unless you just happened to have the average engine and driving conditions every engineer dreams of but never expects.

If you buy the kit from Crane Cams for your GM engine, you will also find inside some springs for tailoring the centrifugal advance curve. Installation and adjustment are easy if you just follow the instructions.

If you have any questions about selecting and equipping your tow vehicle, gearing, etc., write to me at the publisher's address. Include a business-size stamped, self-addressed envelope.

Chapter 19

PullRite Hitch Test Report

For years, I wanted the benefits of a fifth-wheel trailer --no sway, easy maneuvering, uncomplicated hitching -- but I needed a van for other uses and couldn't afford to swap my conventional trailer. Then at an RV show, I saw an exhibit of the PullRite hitch. Apparently it had been around for a several years, but I hadn't seen it or any mention of it.

The hitch is quite innovative in that it uses a swinging drawbar that pivots at a point just behind the axle of the tow vehicle. A ball head and equalizing bars a bit different from Reese-type hitches lock the hitch vertically, except for the limited action allowed by the bars. The equalizing bars bear against steel plates attached to the trailer frame and prohibit any horizontal motion at the ball head.

In effect, the trailer frame and the swinging drawbar become a solid unit except for the vertical motion allowed by the equalizing bars. The drawbar permits a pivot arc of 140 degrees. The company claims many of the towing advantages of fifth-wheels with a conventional travel trailer and any van or pickup. Sway and response to wind and trucks are claimed to be eliminated. Also claimed are shorter turning radius, predictable emergency handling and generally improved towing behavior.

With all other equalizing hitches, the pivot point between trailer and tow vehicle is located at the ball head four or five feet behind the tow vehicle axle. This gives the trailer a lever of four or five feet to use against the tow vehicle. Any movement the trailer makes in response to side winds or passing vehicles translates through that lever to the tow vehicle. As anyone who has towed a trailer can tell you, the result can vary from annoying to terrifying.

PULLRITE AVOIDS SWAY

I suspect that a large number of RVers have bought motorhomes as a direct result of being frightened by trailer sway. Even the use of sway bars does not completely avoid the problem. Emergency maneuvers such as might be needed to avoid another motorist or quickly pull back into a lane induce sway that has put more than one trailer and its tow vehicle into the ditch or worse.

The PullRite hitch avoids all that by placing the pivot point just behind the rear axle of the tow vehicle. This reduces the lever to just a few inches, not enough to be significant. The reduction in lever length is the main reason fifth-wheels tow so well. The trailer can't steer the tow vehicle.

I decided to test the PullRite hitch and see whether its claims were justified. Since the company also claims "complete bolt-on attachment," I also decided to mount the hitch to my van myself. I had previously mounted a couple of Reese-type hitches and felt competent.

When I picked up the package at a local dealer, I had my first intimation that this was going to be a bit different. The PullRite platform is big. And it's heavy. I estimate that the platform and swinging drawbar weigh at least twice as much as a Reese or Valley system. I had assumed that the platform attached to existing holes in the van frame. Wrong! Mounting calls for lifting the platform into place with a floor jack, locating it rather precisely, and drilling six half-inch holes for the attaching bolts.

I did it and saved myself some bucks in the process, but I wouldn't do it again, nor would I advise anyone to try it. The directions are clear and easy to follow, but that's a lot of steel to push around, and half-inch holes aren't easy to drill with the average homeowner's drill.

THE FIRST ROAD TEST

With the hitch in place and a new wiring harness hooked up, it was time for a towing test. Hitching up is much easier than any other hitch I have used in 25 years of trailering. With the ball head attached and the drawbar swung to center, I could easily see the ball and the trailer hitch socket. Pickups wouldn't have it quite so easy, but PullRite suggests if space permits that you swing the bar to the extreme left. Then you can see the ball and hitch past the side of the tow vehicle and easily back into place.

Following the clear directions, I made preliminary adjustments to the equalizing bars and headed for a paved, level parking lot for checking to be sure the trailer and tow vehicle were both level. Final adjustments were easily made in just a few minutes.

I could have chosen a better day for the test, but I was impatient. The wind was blowing hard with gusts running to about 25 mph. I would quickly know whether the hitch eliminated sway. Leaving the parking lot immediately brought out a few differences from other hitches. As I turned, a glance in the mirror showed the trailer far over to one side instead of being directly behind. That would take a bit of getting used to. Another glance also showed that curbs would have to be watched a bit closer. The trailer does cut corners more than with other hitches. That's not a problem. It just calls for some adjustments.

When I reached the expressway and joined heavy traffic, the PullRite really began to show its stuff. Even with those stiff winds from the side, there was absolutely no sway. A gust would simply move the van and trailer as a unit. Correction was no more than if I had not had the trailer.

WHAT ABOUT PASSING TRUCKS?

I started hunting for a semi. I watched carefully when the first one passed. No movement. None. When the next one appeared in the mirror, I deliberately avoided watching. I wanted to see if I could detect by feel when it overtook the trailer. Not a thing! After all the years of being super alert to passing trucks, I was shocked to notice no effect at all. That was why I had bought the hitch. It had passed the main test.

After cruising the expressway for a while to make sure that my first impression was correct -- it was -- I headed back for the lot where I kept the trailer. There was one more test. How would it respond when backing. The pivot point was in a totally different location and backing would be different.

That is the best word to describe it -- different. Backing response seemed to be slower, more like the semi I drove years ago. Parking would take some adjustments.

There are other factors that are not so easily evaluated. PullRite claims a better ride due to reduced pitching leverage. I'm not sure that I could detect any significant difference. But my van had a long wheelbase and wasn't very sensitive to pitch. The reduced leverage would seem to make for a smoother ride on roads that would otherwise produce pitch. I have to admit that the ride was good.

SOME UNEXPECTED BENEFITS

I also admit that I felt more relaxed while driving. There was no feeling of the tail wagging the dog. Trucks and other traffic weren't a problem. Quick maneuvers didn't translate into momentum-induced oscillations. The PullRite hitch made hitch weight less important, so I moved the small motorcycle I carried on the front of the van to the rear of the trailer. I had tried carrying it there with my other hitch, but the added weight on the rear of the trailer produced increased sway. With the PullRite, that was no longer true. Wonderful! I had never liked carrying the motorcycle on the front of the van.

Another benefit is the decreased turning radius. With the swinging drawbar, there is no way that any part of the tow vehicle can touch the trailer. You can turn as sharply as you wish without worrying about bruising either vehicle. The position of the two vehicles is always very clear in the side mirror. Making U-turns on most residential streets becomes a possibility because you can usually back against the turn to further decrease turning radius.

By now you have probably realized I like the PullRite hitch. It isn't perfect. Nothing is. But I surely do like the feeling of confidence that comes from not having to deal with trailer sway. List price at the time of writing is $690. Installation is extra. The dealer I bought mine from charges $60. If you bought your present hitch several years ago, that $690 may seem steep, but the price of other hitches has gone up, Old Buddy. The PullRite is still a little more expensive. But, remember, the hitch is all you need -- no sway bars. When you figure in that savings, the price is very comparable to that of other hitches. Add in the peace of mind and you may decide it is a bargain.

For additional information and the name of your nearest dealer contact:

Pulliam Enterprises, Inc.
55850 Francis Avenue
Mishawaka, IN 46545
(219)259-1520

Chapter 20

RV Length -- What Size is Best?

Never have the choices in RVs been so great. In trailers, there is everything from tiny 13-footers to giants of 40 feet. In motorhomes, the choices range from converted vans and micro-minis of 17 feet to monsters stretching 40 feet with an empty weight in excess of 41,000 pounds. Surely there is something for everyone in there somewhere. But where? What can a 13-foot trailer offer? Why spend $400,000 for a motorhome as large as a bus? What features come with increasing size? And are there any disadvantages other than purchase cost in buying larger?

Answering those questions in the next 1,500 words is a big order, but Ye Editor said, "Do it, Buster, or no royalties check." Persuasive argument!

Let's start small and work our way up. What can a 13-foot RV offer? Well, how about economy in both purchase price and operation? Trailers that length can be towed by most cars and mini-trucks with engines of around 1.7-liter displacement if the owners will help a bit. I towed a 13-footer for thousands of miles with a 1962 six-cylinder Ford Falcon. The miles included many through the Smokies. Most of the micro-mini motorhomes are around 18 to 22 feet, and many of those work well with 2.4-liter engines. A small budget for RVing is no handicap. These small rigs deliver excellent fuel mileage and minimal maintenance expense.

Another advantage of small RVs is their maneuverability. True, short-wheelbase trailers can offer a challenge when backing, but they will follow almost in the tow vehicle's tracks. They are usually only seven feet wide or even less. Small RVs can be parked in some of the most delightful sites that the rest of us must pass up. I most enjoy camping in the various state and national forest campgrounds. In the western mountains many of these campgrounds are restricted to RVs less than 18 feet long.

FEATURES IN SMALL TRAILERS

But how about features? Well, I'm looking at floorplans of a couple of 13-foot trailers. Both offer sleeping space for at least three people, a gas/electric refrigerator, gas oven, more storage space than you would expect, furnace, a water system and a portable toilet as an option. Sorry, no shower until about 16 feet. Some 13-foot models can increase sleeping capacity to four with a fold-out upper bunk. Through camping with youngsters, I've found that most of them prefer sleeping outside in a tent by the time they are 9 or 10 years old.

Moving up the sizes, 16-footers offer optional showers and toilets with larger water systems to match. At about that size, the kitchen range gets an oven and the refrigerator grows a bit to about 4 cubic feet. Sleeping space has also increased in some models to an unbelievable six. To be honest, some of those six had better be small, but four adults can be quite comfortable in a 16-foot trailer. Storage space includes a closet for hanging coats and lots of drawers and under-the-seat compartments.

Micro-mini motorhomes and 18 to 22-foot trailers offer about the same amount of space. Each will have the same features as the 16-footer, but everything gets a little roomier. The beds are larger; six adult-sized sleepers often can be accommodated. The refrigerator demands less frequent trips to the store. Water storage is greater. The shower has grown to include that strange object, the sit tub. And very important to some people, floor space has increased.

Because of the necessity to include an engine and front seats in micro-minis, floor space is still more constricted than in a trailer of the same size. When cars had stronger frames and could support greater hitch weight, trailers didn't acquire tandem axles until about 23 feet. Tandem axles are now common in even 18-foot trailers and not unknown in 16-footers.

PERMANENT BEDS APPEAR

Except for the strange bed in the cab-over section of micro-minis, permanent beds don't appear until the RV stretches to 24 feet. One popular 24-foot trailer floor plan has a front kitchen and dinette, center living area with folding couch/bed and rear bedroom with bath. With two hanging closets and loads of drawers and compartments, the model offers long-term livability for all but the most unreformed pack rats.

For families needing mucho sleeping space, some 22-foot RVs offer beds for up to eight. In some models, some of the beds will be slings or fold-downs, but they are beds. Others have permanent bunks plus the couch/bed and convertible dinette. Permanent bunks do take their toll in floor space, however.

From 26 feet and up, increasing space is the most noticeable factor. Everything gets larger. A permanent bed or twin beds is universal. The bath will likely have a nearly home-size tub and dressing space. Closets hold enough clothes for full-time living. The living area will have a comfortable couch and one or two lounge chairs. A dedicated TV shelf appears. There are sufficient drawers for all the little things. The galley -- that's the kitchen for all you lot-bound types -- will have a double sink, an 8 or 10 cubic foot refrigerator, plenty of storage space, a separate pantry for canned and boxed foods, a microwave oven and ample counter space to prepare food for more people than you want. The dinette will seat up to six with additional dining space at a fold-up table by the couch. The floor will be carpeted from end to end, and picture windows on both sides of the living area will offer pleasant views of your surroundings. What more could you ask?

Well, apparently some people do ask more, so the RVs keep growing. At around 32 feet, space for a washer-dryer combination is an option. There is more closet space for guess who. Some models offer two separate bedrooms with queen-size or twin beds. The living area may have a slide-out room addition, offering enough space for a cocktail party. Well, a small one. Many RVers will install an electric organ or piano or small stereo. Some models have enough space for part of it to be an office or studio for writers and artists. Portable photography darkrooms are not unknown.

For those of us who started with 13-footers, the space in a 35-foot RV can be intimidating. For full-timers, RVs this size can offer almost all the comforts of home.

THE PRICE INCREASES WITH SIZE

What prices do the increasing sizes exact? Well, maneuverability and campsite restrictions have already been mentioned. But there is obviously more. In today's market with anemic cars and trucks, weight is an important factor. Both Ford and GM offer a few models of cars rated to pull up to 5,000 pounds. Let me state my case clearly. There is no car built today that can adequately tow a 5000-pound trailer.

With the exception of motorhomes with large diesel engines, weight is definitely a factor to be considered. The dry or empty weight of RVs is frequently quoted in sales literature. Nothing is said about the loaded weight. The loaded weight of RVs tends to increase by about 25% to 50% of the empty weight, with the larger RVs growing the most. As my mail indicates on a daily basis, weight is a serious problem.

Trailers up to 15 feet tend to have dry weights under 2,000 pounds. Some weigh as little as 1,200 pounds. Add 25% for propane, water, food, clothing, and personal items and the weight has grown to 1,500 or 2,500 pounds. Many small cars are limited by the manufacturer to 2,000 pounds of trailer. That's loaded weight. And that doesn't say that the car can perform well with the trailer.

By the time a trailer has grown to 24 feet, its loaded weight has reached 5,500 to 6,000 lbs. Trailers that size require a van or full-size pickup truck with a 5.7-liter engine and optional gearing. Motorhomes that size will all have 5.7-liter engines or larger. A 35-foot trailer will have a loaded weight of 9,500 pounds or more. Motorhomes that length hit the scales at around 14,000 pounds unless they are the luxury models. Those monsters climb to the 40-foot behemoth mentioned earlier with an empty weight of over 41,000 pounds. Fortunately, loaded weight of RVs tends to stop increasing once each resident has loaded about 1,000 pounds.

The really large Class A motorhomes all have diesel engines commonly found in over-the-road trucks. At around 15,000 pounds, there are no gasoline engines capable of giving adequate performance.

FUEL COSTS, PURCHASE PRICES

Another price exacted by size is the cost of fuel. Micro-minis and small trailers may deliver as much as 18 mpg. That makes for very economical travel. Mileage with Class C motorhomes and 25-foot trailers commonly runs around 8 to 10 mpg. Larger gasoline powered RVs gulp fuel at 5 to 9 mpg. A diesel engine can increase that by 50%. Large diesel-powered Class A motorhomes give around 7 to 11 mpg. Clearly, fuel costs can become a significant factor.

Purchase price can't be forgotten, either. A 13-foot trailer may have a list price under $4,000. Micro-mini motorhomes list from just under $16,000 to $29,000. Mid-size trailers, 24-footers, list for $7,000 to $13,000. From there, the prices rise to a top of around $50,000 for travel trailers, up to $85,000 for fifth-wheels and over $400,000 for top-of-the-line Class A motorhomes.

By definition, RVs mean mobility. Mobility decreases as size increases. For each family, there is an optimum size. I have friends who swear by their 35-foot Class A motorhome. But they live in it full time. And they started out smaller, buying larger only as they determined their new life style. Others I've seen live full time in 24-foot trailers or 27-foot Class C motorhomes.

The wide range of sizes makes the choice at once easy and difficult. There is a size for each of us. A family starting on a small budget will find their needs met by an equally small-budget RV. As family size, amount of leisure time, type of use and budget change, there will be a different size that is best.

A favorite pasttime for RVers is visiting the shows. Some are looking for a reason to trade. Others are looking for assurance that they already have the best RV. And that's the way it should be.

Chapter 21

Selecting Spark Plugs and Ignition Coil

Christopher Jacobs, one of the leading experts on ignition systems in the United States, says that the correct ignition is the most critical component on your gasoline engine. Choosing the right spark plugs, the appropriate gap, the correct ignition coil and spark plug wires can probably make a greater improvement in the way your engine runs than any other similar expenditure.

In a previous chapter (Power Tuning Your Engine), I gave suggestions for adjusting the ignition timing to improve performance. This time we'll take a look at how you can make additional improvements through proper selection of your ignition coil, spark plug wires and spark plugs. I've seen gains as high as 13% in a previously well-tuned engine just by proper selection of these three components. Obviously, I can't promise the same, but I can promise some improvement.

When your engine left the factory, it was equipped with the infamous compromise system. The engineers designed the engine for a hypothetical average driver and average conditions. RVing is far from an average condition. It follows that selecting ignition components for our special conditions will result in improved performance. How much improvement? That depends upon just how far your use deviates from average.

Let's start with the ignition coil. Most of us seldom even look at the coil, let alone know what it does. But the coil is very important to your engine's performance. Without a properly operating ignition coil, the engine won't run. The coil's main job is to convert the 12 volts supplied by the battery to spark energy at the plugs.

COIL ACTS LIKE TRANSFORMER

If the spark has enough energy and occurs at the right time, the air-fuel mixture in the cylinder will burn and the engine will produce power. But 12 volts won't jump the spark plug gap. The coil acts like a transformer, increasing the voltage to 12,000 to 20,000 or more volts. In a modern engine, 12,000 volts is enough to cause the spark. Engineers design some reserve energy so that the spark will occur even if the fuel mixture is a little too rich or there is some oil-fouling or any of the other negative conditions exist.

So, if 12,000 volts is enough under most conditions, wouldn't 40,000 volts be better? There's that good, old American idea that if a little is good, a lot has to be better. In this case, it doesn't work. I won't ask you to remember your high school physics lessons on transformers. I'll just remind you that voltage and amperage are the two electrical properties that transformers work with. And I'll remind you that they work inversely through a transformer. When one goes up, the other comes down. High output voltage means lower output amperage. So what? What's the big deal?

The big deal is that voltage doesn't ignite the fuel; amperage does. You could have a spark at a million volts and very low amperage and the spark wouldn't ignite the fuel. So what you want is a coil that puts out enough voltage to cause a spark with lots of amperage. The best way to get that is to select a coil with an output of around 20,000 volts. Forget the "high energy 40,000-volt super blasters" at the speed shop. You're better off with what came from the factory.

There are some coils that are designed to tailor the output energy to what's happening in the combustion chambers. These have a core that is variably permeable. The variable permeability lets the coil furnish an extra hot spark when needed, such as when starting the engine or when the plug starts to foul, then cools the spark down a bit when the engine is hot. Look for a coil that is described as being "automatically controlled". The Jacobs Compu*Coil from Jacobs Electrical Products (3327 Verdugo Road, Los Angeles, CA 90065) is an example. Coils by Accel and Mallory are also good, but don't go for the high-voltage models.

METAL COIL CASE IS BEST

Look for a coil with a metal case. Transformers generate a lot of heat when they work. If the heat isn't dissipated, the coil can't work. A metal case conducts the heat better than a plastic case. For the same reason, select a coil filled with fluid. The tower where the high tension lead plugs in should be rippled instead of smooth. The ripples supply a longer path and greater resistance for the electricity that is trying to escape. That means more energy gets to the plugs. Buy a coil that is advertised to have high amperage and work with a large spark plug gap. We'll get to that later.

When the coil releases its energy into the high-tension wires, the energy is on its way to the spark plug. Unfortunately, some of it won't get there. Leaky wires are the bane of modern gasoline engines. Spark plug wires that have cheap insulation, are mishandled or are too close to exhaust manifolds let some or all of that important electrical energy escape. Electrical energy that doesn't get to the spark plugs is a waste.

Look for spark plug wires with a silicone insulation, vulcanized spark plug boots and a ferrite or impregnated core with a fine wire spirally wound around the core. Then be sure the wires are carefully installed. The manufacturer did one thing very right in figuring the best place for the wires to travel. Put your new ones in the same place. Be sure they are clear of hot spots and free from mechanical stress.

At the business end of each spark plug wire is the spark plug. The spark plug operates in a very hostile environment and has to do its work in milli-seconds under very high pressure. If it is oil-fouled or the gap isn't correct for the type of service or the heat range is wrong, the engine wastes fuel and doesn't generate its rated power.

THOSE COMPROMISES AGAIN

The spark plug's only purpose is to ignite the fuel mixture. The engineers placed the plug tip as near as possible to the spot in the combustion chamber. But here is where an important set of compromises gets in the way. The engineer works to an expense budget as well as a set of operating assumptions. The ignition coil he selects is not the best one for the job, but it fits the budget. He has to select a plug gap that will work with the coil output. The theoretical best gap would be .100-inch, but the ignition system won't support a gap that large. The resistance is just too great, and the spark will find other ways to escape with less resistance. On some engines, GMs prior to the latest models are an example, the spark will burn a hole through the distributor rotor rather than jump a large gap at the plugs.

Selecting the optimum plug gap is a process of trial. Start with the factory recommended gap and run a power test. One way is to carefully measure the full-throttle acceleration time between two posts approximately 100 yards apart. Then open the plug gaps .010 inch and repeat the tests. Continue until the power falls off. The previously tested gap is optimum for your engine. On my Ford 460, I found that my best power and mileage was obtained with a gap of .080 inch. The factory recommended gap was .044 inch. That's quite a difference, but the improvement in power was very noticeable.

Although I never experienced any problems -- I found no significant increase in gap after 20,000 miles -- some engines will erode the plug gap rapidly enough that they need to be checked more frequently. An electrical spark jumps with less resistance when the electrode edges are sharp. Each spark jump tears off a microscopic bit of metal from the electrodes. After thousands of miles, the electrodes are no longer sharp as they were when new. The rounded edges require greater voltage to make the jump even if the gap remained the same.

But the gap doesn't remain the same. As the metal is torn off, some of it is blown out the exhaust with the burnt gases. Due to variations in electrode metals, some brands of spark plugs erode more slowly than others. Motorcraft and Autolite plugs seem to resist electrode erosion better than others.

SPARK PLUG CHOICE

When it comes time to replace plugs, most owners either leave the choice of brand and type to the mechanic or simply follow the factory recommendations. That's okay if your driving meets the criteria of average as arrived at by the factory engineers, but we've already agreed that our driving is not average. Most of our engines would be happier with a different spark plug.

The most important thing to consider is heat range. Combustion temperatures under heavy loads can be very high. The spark plug tip is right in the middle of that heat and gets very hot. If the heat were not dissipated, the plug tip would continue getting hotter until it melted. But the plug works best when the tip remains at around 700 degrees. If it gets hotter, it may glow and cause detonation. That can ruin your whole week. If the plug runs as cool as 300 degrees -- some cool! -- it is likely to foul from lubricating oil or products of combustion. So the tip heat must be carefully controlled. As you might imagine, the engineers have figured out a way.

The heat absorbed by the plug tip flows up the extended porcelain until it reaches the metal base. From there, it flows into the cylinder head and is absorbed by the coolant. The longer the path, the hotter the tip will be. Hot plugs have longer porcelain extensions. Also, hot plugs have narrower porcelain tips to absorb heat more slowly. The problem is to balance the engine load against the cooling capacity of the plug. Again, it's trial and error.

Take a look at your plugs after driving under load for an hour. If the heat range is correct, the porcelain should be free from oil or carbon deposits with a light tan or gray color. If the porcelain is white and has a blistered appearance, the plugs are running too hot. Have your parts man select the next cooler heat range. If the plugs are oil- or carbon-fouled, a hotter plug may help to correct the problem. Oil fouling indicates poor oil control from worn rings, leaking valve stems or seals, or a plugged PCV valve. If your engine is in good mechanical condition, most RV engines can use a spark plug one step cooler than normal.

The heart of your RV engine is its ignition system. If the ignition system isn't working at peak efficiency, your engine is delivering less power and mileage than it should. Your time and a few bucks can make a difference.

Chapter 22

Technical Terms Explained

There is one thing a technical writer can depend upon. Sooner or later, he is going to write something that is not understood.

An unfortunate fact of life is that not all of us have the same vocabulary. Each of us is educated in his own way and accumulates a set of terms which, though common to him, may be strange to someone else. Writers have to face this problem with every word they write. We want to be understood. But we also have to make some assumptions about our readers. We can't start back in kindergarten with every article. There isn't enough editorial space.

But every so often it may be necessary to draw back and give an expanded glossary of terms. That's what this chapter is about. A magazine reader complained very properly that without an explanation of terms, the technical articles he read were meaningless. He listed several terms and statements that had appeared in a recent magazine by three technical writers. Somehow, an editor decided I should be the one to try and explain. Am I being punished? I'll take each of the terms and try to explain them.

• ***What is a power converter?***

Nearly all RVs built in the last 10 years use a 12-volt battery to supply electrical power for such things as lights, ventilating fans, furnace fan and ignition of the refrigerator and furnace. There is also a separate electrical system furnishing 120 volts through normal wall plates for the air conditioner and hair dryers and such. Obviously, there will be no power to the 120-volt system unless the RV is plugged into the power system of the campground or you are using your own generator. Until several years ago, the two electrical systems were completely separate. Then some brainy type figured out that a device similar to a battery charger could be used to recharge the 12-volt battery when the RV was plugged into the campground power. A few modifications later, and the power converter was born. It's simply a device that converts 120 volts alternating current (AC) into 12-volt direct current (DC) to keep the battery fully charged. Nearly every RV has one. It's operation is automatic.

• *What is specific gravity?*

This is a term from physics and chemistry. Centuries ago, it was discovered that a heavy object immersed in water displaced an amount of water equal in volume to the immersed object. If the amount of water displaced was weighed, it could be compared with the weight of the object. For example, if I weigh 200 pounds and displace 210 pounds of water in a tub or barrel, the weight of my volume of water can be compared with my body weight.

The weight of the object divided by the weight of the displaced water is called the object's specific gravity. In the example, my specific gravity would be .95. The specific gravity of fluids can also be computed. In the article the writer referred to, specific gravity was used in reference to the fluid in a battery. A useful property of battery fluid is that when the battery is fully charged, the fluid is heavier than when the battery is discharged. So checking the specific gravity of a battery with a device called a hydrometer is one way to determine the level of charge in a battery. (Hey, I didn't say it was going to be easy!)

• *What are 12VDC terminals?*

Unfortunately, some of us fall back on a form of shorthand when writing or talking. VDC is shorthand for volts direct current. Most vehicles other than some large trucks and airplanes use 12-volt batteries. Batteries can supply only direct current. (Please don't ask me to explain the difference between direct and alternating current. The publisher wouldn't stand for my using that much space.) So we commonly refer to battery power as 12VDC. The connecting points on batteries and other electrical devices are called terminals. They are just the points where wires are connected. So 12VDC terminals are the connecting points on batteries or other parts of the 12-volt system in the RV. Since a power converter is connected to 120 volts and supplies 12 volts direct current, it has both 120VAC and 12VDC terminals.

• *What is a relay and what does it look like?*

A relay is a remote electrical switch that uses a small amount of power to switch a large amount of power. Large amounts of power require heavy wire. It is often uneconomical or inconvenient to run heavy wire to the operator's location. So a light wire carrying a small amount of power is run to that location. Turning on a small switch activates a larger switch in the high power section. A relay is also used in a power converter to control power through the various parts of the converter. A relay can take different physical forms, so it's tough to describe what one looks like. Often, they are cylindrical in shape with two small and two large wires connected to their corresponding terminals. Frankly, I don't know why you would be looking for one. Trouble-shooting a power converter is probably a job for a trained technician, and he would know what he is looking for.

• *What are DC devices?*

As mentioned above, DC refers to direct current. DC devices are pieces of electrical equipment that operate on direct current. In an RV, they are the 12-volt lights and fans on the furnace and the ventilating hood in the bathroom. Some people also use 12-volt hair curling irons and dryers and some small kitchen appliances. These are 12-volt DC devices.

•What will I see when I turn a circuit breaker to "off" to know that the relay de-energizes? What does "de-energize" mean?

Circuit breakers have almost universally replaced fuse boxes in homes and RVs. They are safety devices that break the circuit instantly when the circuit is overloaded or carrying too much current from a short circuit. There is usually more than one circuit or series of electrical outlets in an RV. Each circuit is protected by its own breaker.

On the front of the box containing the breakers are levers or rockers or some sort of handle so that the individual breakers can be manually operated just like a switch. There will be at least two positions for the switch handle, "on" and "off." Moving the handle to off breaks the electrical current throughout that circuit. Since supplying power to a relay is termed "energizing" the relay, breaking the circuit will "de-energize" the relay. If the breaker handle is moved to its "off" position, the relay is de-energized.

•How can I "check for voltage on the coil" and how do I check for voltage and where and what is the coil?

Voltage is checked with a voltmeter. One can be purchased from stores such as Radio Shack if you really want one. Voltage is checked by first setting the control on the voltmeter to the proper scale for the expected voltage. That is, set it for either DC or AC and the range of voltage being measured. Usually, small meters will have a DC range that runs from 0 to 25 volts and an AC range from 0 to 500 volts. There will be other ranges, but those are the ones you will be interested in.

There will be two wires coming from the meter with metal probes on the opposite ends. Placing a probe on the terminals of the device being checked will let you measure the voltage running through the device. In checking DC voltage, if the meter reading shows less than zero, reverse the probes. Since I didn't write the article the reader refers to and don't have a copy of it, I don't know what coil is referred to. I suspect from the context of the letter that the article was discussing power converters. Again, unless you know what you're doing, you had better leave trouble-shooting the power converter to someone else.

• *What is a burnishing file?*

There are electrical contact points in a relay that open and close to turn the current off and on in the controlled circuit. Those points can become corroded through exposure to the air. They can also become burned from the small electrical arcing or sparking that occurs each time the relay is energized. Over a period of time, the burning or corrosion can become so severe that current will no longer flow. The burning or corrosion needs to be removed. A burnishing file is a file with very fine teeth that is used to clean the points.

• *How do I "measure the voltage on the relay's terminals"?*

The relay in the power converter (if you found it) has two sets of terminals, 12VDC and 120VAC. The 12VDC terminals are the ones you are interested in. A heavy white wire will run from one terminal to a junction bar with a lot of other white wires. That is the positive or "+" terminal. There will also be a similar black wire running from the relay. That is the ground, negative, or "-" wire. With the scale on your voltmeter set on the smallest range that includes 12 volts, touch the red wire probe from the meter to the bare end of the positive wire or its terminal. Touch the black wire probe from the meter to a similar point on the ground wire from the relay. The meter should register about 13 volts if it is working correctly and the RV is plugged into the campground (or your home) electrical system.

• *What are the relay connectors?*

Those are the terminals on the relay where the wires mentioned above connect.

• *What is a converter?*

In the context of the article, it is the power converter. Sometimes we get lazy and omit the complete terminology. Even physicians do. They say a person had a cardiac when they mean he had a cardiac arrest. Would it be clearer to say "His heart stopped"? Accountants also shorten "accounts receivable" to "receivables." (I just thought I'd throw that in to show that we technical writers are not the only ones who confuse people.)

• ***What are "13 volts charger output"?***

A battery charger or a power converter puts out direct current (DC) at a rate high enough to charge the battery. Since a fully charged 12-volt battery will usually register about 12.6 volts, the charger will have to develop greater voltage or it won't "push" voltage into the battery and recharge it. Battery chargers typically develop 13 to 15 volts. That is the charger output.

• ***What is a digital voltmeter?***

Most older and a few new voltmeters have the familiar scale with a moving needle. Digital voltmeters instead display the meter reading on a screen using numerals or "digits." Some instrument displays in new cars and trucks use a digital display. Many people wear watches with digital displays. The old watches and instruments with moving needles were called analog displays. The term "analog" comes from the dial and needle displays being an analogy or representation of the action being measured.

• ***What are diodes?***

Diodes are tiny electrical devices with only two connectors that permit electricity to flow through in only one direction. Plumbing systems use a similar device called a check valve to let fluids flow in one direction. A diode is an electrical check valve.

• ***What is a transformer?***

A transformer is an electrical device that changes an incoming electrical current to a different value. It uses two sets of wire windings with a different number of windings in each set. Depending upon the way the transformer is hooked up, the output can have a greater or lesser voltage than the input. In the power converter of RVs, a transformer is used to reduce incoming 120VAC to an output of 12VAC. Another part of the converter "converts" the 12VAC to 12VDC.

• ***What is a "regulator circuit board"?***

That's the part of the power converter that makes certain the electrical output stays within certain limits. If it were not for the regulator, the electrical output could vary from too low voltage to too high voltage. There are many ways to regulate output. Some are mechanical. Modern converters use a circuit board, which is a small board holding several electronic devices working together to accomplish, in this case, a carefully controlled flow of electricity.

• *What is a torque converter?*

There are two main sections of an automatic transmission. The rear section contains gears and clutches which accomplish the gear speed changes. The gears are hooked directly through the drive shaft to the rear wheels. When the car is sitting still with the engine running, the gears don't turn. The torque converter is a fluid connection between the engine and the gear section of the transmission. It operates much like two electric fans that sit facing each other with one plugged into the outlet box and the other not. If you hold the blades of the one not plugged in, it won't turn. Release the blades, and the flow of air from the running fan will cause the blades of the other fan to turn.

In a transmission, the blades of the torque converter are completely surrounded by transmission fluid to transmit the force very efficiently. As you might suspect, the blades of a torque converter are shaped rather differently from the blades of an electric fan.

A torque converter also acts like an infinitely variable gear reduction device. It gives a large gear reduction when the vehicle first starts moving. As the vehicle accelerates, the two parts of the converter slowly assume the same speed. Under cruising conditions, the torque converter has little or no slippage for zero gear reduction. It is this gear reduction property of the torque converter that gives automatic transmissions superior load starting ability.

• *How does a person install a transmission temperature gauge?*

Because of slippage in the torque converter section of the transmission, a lot of heat is generated. If the heat becomes extreme -- over 250 degrees for an extended time -- the transmission can be damaged. To determine whether their transmissions are overheating, some RVers install a gauge to measure the transmission fluid temperature. The gauge itself is mounted somewhere on the dashboard where it can be seen. The "sending unit," the part of the gauge that actually senses the heat, is mounted where it will be continually bathed in transmission fluid. The best mounting place is in a hole drilled in the bottom of the transmission pan or lower cover. Since this will obviously let fluid run out during the installation, it is best done when the fluid is being changed.

Select a spot on the pan that will not let the sending unit interfere with any part of the transmission. Drill a hole to accept the "boss," usually a brass pipe adapter, and braze the boss in place. Brazing is a process similar to welding that is done at a lower heat. Welding is likely to set up stresses in the metal that could cause cracks. The sending unit is screwed into the boss. An insulated wire connects the sending unit to the dash-mounted gauge.

Since mounting the sending unit in the pan may in some instances be inconvenient, many owners insert a pipe "T" in the transmission fluid outlet line. The "T" must be placed as near the transmission as possible. The sending unit can be threaded into the "T."

• *Where is the transmission cooler installed?*

Usually it is mounted in front of the radiator or air conditioner condenser. The cooler will include a mounting kit that makes installation easy. The directions are quite clear and complete. On some vehicles, there may not be room for the cooler at that location. In that case, find a spot where the cooler will receive an unimpeded flow of air but will not be likely to be hit by flying debris from the road or another vehicle. That may have to be in a horizontal position slightly below the radiator. Since the airflow in that position will not be the best, you may then need to use a small electrical radiator cooling fan mounted on the cooler.

• *How do I know the largest transmission cooler that will fit?*

I frequently recommend installing the "largest cooler that will fit." That recommendation gave rise to the above question. Measure the space where you want to mount the cooler. See how long and wide a space you have available. Also check the distance between the radiator and the grill or grill mounting brackets. Most coolers will require an inch of depth. Once you have determined the size of the space available, you can measure the available coolers to find the largest that will fit in the space. As a practical matter, a 23,000-pound cooler from Hayden takes a space 17 inches X 10 inches. There are larger coolers, with some as large as many radiators. These are specialty items for heavy towing or motorhomes. It is my opinion that coolers are rated optimistically. I recommend a cooler rated for twice your gross combined vehicle weight. Any dealer can give you the measurements so that you can determine whether the cooler will fit.

• ***When a dealer says that another transmission cooler would negate the new car warranty, then what?***

The dealer is blowing smoke. No warranty is voided by adding another cooler. If he doesn't want to add the cooler, find someone who will or do it yourself. I can guarantee you that no warranty is voided by adding a transmission cooler. What is likely to happen is that if a transmission is ruined as a result of overheating, the dealer may void the warranty due to abuse of the vehicle. An adequate auxiliary cooler would prevent that.

Chapter 23

Tires: How to Select Them

Selecting the right tires for your RV is a lot more involved than just looking at the size stamped on the side of the old tires and buying new ones with the same numbers. The old ones may have been inadequate for the job, they may have been too small or too large, and they may have been the wrong tread design. It's often possible to correct a bad wear pattern by proper selection of new tires.

Let's look at an example of changing the wear pattern by changing tires. As most of you know, I like Ford trucks and vans. Also, as most of you know, Ford uses a front suspension that is different from any others. The suspension works fine, but with most tires the outside edges wear down earlier than they should. I long ago accepted that as normal on my Fords. Then a few years ago I found an alignment mechanic who also was fond of Fords. He told me to change to Michelin XCH4 tires, and my wear problem would disappear. I thought that was the usual sales talk, but I made the switch. Bingo! No more rapid wearing on the outside edge.

I asked the mechanic what made the difference. He said there were three reasons. One, Fords and most other vans and light trucks need 40 pounds of air pressure. The passenger tires I had been using were load-rated B, and 32 pounds was the maximum rated pressure. The Michelins were load-rated C and would take up to 50 pounds pressure even though 40 pounds was sufficient for the loads I was carrying.

A second reason was the tread design. Most other all-season tires have a course tread pattern extending out to the edges. The course edges gave a rough area for the main contact surface and developed an exaggerated wear pattern that soon developed into small cups. The Michelins had a course pattern except at the edges. The edges were much smoother. The cupping did not develop.

The third reason he gave was that the Michelins used a harder rubber compound and resisted wear better than the passenger tires I had been using.

WEAR PROBLEMS CURED

I'm not a tire engineer, but the Michelins did cure my wear problems. They gave significantly longer wear and seemed to ride better. Ford must think they are better, too. The new Ford truck I just got came with Michelin XCH4 tires.

I'm sure that there are other brands that would do as well. If I were looking at other brands of tires, I would certainly look for tread edges similar to the Michelins. I would also insist on a load range adequate for the load carried. It's tougher to evaluate the grade of rubber being used. You have to depend on the manufacturer's integrity or your personal experience with a brand of tires.

Tire size is easier to deal with. The markings are right on the sidewalls. But they do need some interpretation.

Sizes are marked by several different systems using a combination of metrics, inches and letters. A common system is the metric. A tire might be labeled 205/R15. That means the tire is 205 millimeters wide at its widest point, uses a radial cord system and fits on a rim that is 15 inches in diameter. Or it might be labeled 205/R60-15. That would be the same size tire except that the distance from the rim to the tread is only 60% of the cross section. Although the tires would appear to be the same in total diameter, they aren't. The aspect ratio or ratio of section height to cross section, 60, means that the tire is shorter in total diameter than a tire marked with no aspect ratio. A tire with an aspect ratio of 50 would be still smaller. Most, but not all, of these metric sized tires are used on passenger cars.

Another system of marking is similar but has the marking "P" or "LT" in front. P235/75R15 is a common size. The "P" simply means that the tire is intended for passenger car use and is usually built only in load rate B with a maximum pressure of 32 pounds. "LT" tires are built for light truck use and can have a load rating of C, D or E. These tires can carry higher pressures and much higher loads than "P" marked tires.

DO NOT OVER-INFLATE

An important point that some owners overlook is that even though a tire may be load-rated E and can be inflated to 80 pounds, it does not have to be. Inflate the tire no more than is necessary to carry the load. For example, a common size tire on three-fourths ton trucks is LT235/85R16 in load rating E. Inflated to 80 pounds, each tire can safely carry 3,042 pounds. That's much more than most of us would need on a tow vehicle, for example. Lowering the pressure to 40 pounds would give the tire a capacity of 1,870 pounds or 3,740 pounds for the rear axle. Unless you're carrying a fifth wheel trailer or camper, that would be sufficient for most vans or tow trucks and would give a better ride.

Another tire sizing system uses inches and inches. A tire marked 7.50R16 is an example. The tire is basically round in cross section and section height, 7.5 inches in cross section, radial ply design, and fits a 16-inch rim. This marking system has been used for decades and includes very large tires used on heavy trucks and buses.

Another system of sizing that has become popular uses a marking that includes the outside diameter of the tire. A popular size is 33X12.50R15. The tire has an outside diameter of 33 inches, a cross-section of 12.5 inches, a radial design and fits a 15-inch rim. Obviously, it would be a wider than normal rim.

EXTRA-WIDE TIRES

There is widespread belief that an oversize or extra-wide tire gives better traction and wear than the normal size. In most instances that is true. But the extra-wide or larger-size tire will also have a larger-than-normal diameter and will significantly change your overall gear ratio. One drastic example would be a half-ton truck that came on P235/75R15 tires that the owner replaced with 33X12.50R15 with new, wide wheels. He might also have to enlarge the wheel wells a bit.

The P235s had a diameter of 29.1 inches and the 33s had a diameter of 32.6 inches. (They flatten a bit with load. That's why the diameter isn't the same as marked.) With a gear ratio of 3.73-1 and the original tires, the engine would turn 2,685 rpm at 60 mph. That's a good, efficient engine speed for most of our light truck engines. With the big tires, the engine speed would drop to 2,394 rpm at the same road speed. The engine can't develop as much horsepower and has a shorter lever with which to work. It simply can't pull as well. It would be the same as going to a gear ratio of 3.32-1 with the original tires.

Many truck owners have run into a similar situation with the new trucks they bought recently. For years, they towed with a half-ton truck with a gear ratio of 3.73. They decided to upgrade to three-fourths ton using the same size engine and gear ratio that had worked so well for them. The new truck seems not to have as much power as the old one and they are unhappy. They didn't notice the change in tire sizes. The old truck used P235/75R15 tires, and the new one has LT235/85R16 tires. The old tires had a diameter of 29.1 inches and the new ones are 31.9 inches. That's enough to ruin the overall gear ratio. To maintain the same engine speed and performance, they would need a gear ratio of 4.10-1 in the new truck.

An important factor in buying new tires is the load capacity. A tire that is overloaded is a tire looking for a place to fail. You can bet that the place it chooses won't be convenient for you. Buy tires that can safely carry your load. That means you had better drive the RV across a set of scales. At least weigh each axle separately. Better still is to find the weight on each wheel. That's particularly true of motorhomes.

MATCH TIRES WITH WEIGHT

After you've found the axle weight, start looking for tires with adequate capacity. Suppose your rear axle weighs 4,400 lbs. That's 2,200 pounds per rear tire if you don't have duals. Your LT235/85R16s in load E will carry that much weight with 50 pounds of pressure, and they can be inflated to 80 pounds to carry a weight of 6,084 pounds on the axle. Inflating to 55 pounds would give you an axle rating of 4,670 pounds for bit of safety margin.

You might be able to find the same size tires with a load rating of C. C tires have a maximum inflation pressure of 50 pounds That would give the minimum capacity for your load without the safety margin. Load D tires allow an inflation pressure of 65 pounds. With D rated tires inflated to 55 pounds, you would have the same capacity as with the E rated tires but would have a slightly more flexible tire for a better ride.

Motorhome owners have a bit different situation. When used as duals, tires have a lower capacity. For example, the LT235/85R16s at 85 pounds have a capacity of 3,042 pounds when used as singles. As duals, the capacity drops to 2,778 lbs. A set of duals in that size has an axle capacity of 11,112 lbs. But most Class C motorhomes don't use tires that large. Many older Class C's are fitted with 8.75R16.5 tires in load range D. Maximum axle capacity is 8,280 pounds for duals.

If you have that size tires, you may be in for an unpleasant surprise. Weigh your rig's rear axle and see. Newer Class C's built on the Ford chassis are likely to be fitted with for LT215/85R16 tires for an axle capacity of 8,600 pounds. That would be an easy figure to overload. Ford rates the rear axle at 8,000 pounds. Better weigh yours.

Many trailers are fitted with tires using an older alphanumeric size marking. Tires marked F78X15 or something similar are common. The letter indicates the cross-section, with letters farther up the alphabet being larger. The 78 is the aspect ratio and the final number indicates the rim size in inches. Tires built for trailers are about the only ones still using this marking system. If you need a replacement tire in North Tulles, Wyoming, you may have trouble. You might try and find a passenger tire the same diameter. For example, Sears says the F78X15 can be replaced with P205/75, P215/70, P215/65, P235/60, or P245/50. Similar size replacements are available for other alphanumeric size tires.

A large problem still exists, however. Almost without exception, the P- replacements are load-rated B, and many trailers need load-rated C tires. If that is the case with your trailer, it would be dangerous to use the B-rated tires. You will have to look for C-rated tires of the right size.

BIAS PLY OR RADIAL?

Another question arises when it's time to replace all of the trailer tires. Should the replacements be bias ply or radial ply? Although this is changing, most trailers come from the factory with bias ply tires. They are less expensive, and they work well. But nearly all tow vehicles, cars and motorhomes come with radial ply tires because of their superior wear, traction and fuel mileage characteristics. Shouldn't these same characteristics be important in trailer tires?

The evidence is unclear. Very few owners have tried radial tires on trailers, and even fewer have made the results of their experiences known. Certainly, the radial characteristics are just as valid for a trailer as for a tow vehicle. Some owners have argued that the more flexible sidewalls of radial ply tires would increase the trailer's tendency to sway. Others have argued just as vehemently on the opposite side of the question. I tend to believe that radials would not increase the tendency to sway in most instances, but I have not tested the notion simply because I have not had to replace all the tires on a trailer for many, many years.

Goodyear has developed a line of radial ply trailer tires. When I talked with a Goodyear dealer, he said that the company had no reported problems with the tires. By now there may be other companies with similar tires.

As for motorhomes and tow vehicles, there is no question in my mind. Radials are superior to bias ply tires. Handling is much improved on difficult pavement that has been rutted by heavy trucks. Radial ply tires give more miles before needing replacement. And they increase fuel mileage and traction.

RIM FAILURE POSSIBLE

If you have an older vehicle, there is one caution. Some older wheels were not designed to withstand the greater sideloads on the rims that are imposed by radial ply tires. There have been several instances of rim failure when radial ply tires were installed on these older wheels. Have your tire dealer check yours.

A couple of final points about inflation pressure need to be made. Pressures should be checked at least once a week when the tires are cool. That means before the vehicle is driven. Make a note of the number of pounds each tire is low and add that much when you get to the tire pump. If it's necessary to check the tires when warm, expect pressures to be three to five pounds higher than when cool. Never release pressure from a hot tire. It is hot because it has been flexing from being underinflated. Releasing pressure just makes the situation worse.

When a tire is properly inflated, the tread touches the pavement evenly from edge to edge. An underinflated tire tends to run on the edges with the center receiving little contact. An overinflated tire tends to run on the center with the edges making little contact.

This gives rise to a simple system for determining the correct pressure for your tires. With soft chalk draw a broad line across the tread of each tire from edge to edge. Drive straight ahead several feet on smooth pavement and inspect the marks. If the inflation pressure is correct, the chalk mark will be evenly worn off from edge to edge. If the center shows more wear, the inflation pressure is too high. If the edges show more wear, the pressure is too low.

Proper selection of tires and correct inflation will add miles to their wear and make driving a pleasure. It pays to take the time to do it right.

Chapter 24

Tire Size Makes A Difference

As long as your tires are large enough to carry the load safely, does it make any difference what size they are? Let's look at some figures.

The two most common size light truck and van tires are LT235/75-15 and LT235/85-16. The numbers look about the same, don't they? A lot of truck buyers apparently think so, too. Judging from the sales literature from the truck manufacturers, they agree. That kind of error can get you into deep trouble.

If you read my articles regularly, you know that I put a lot of emphasis on gearing for the right engine speed. The best economy and performance can be obtained when the engine is properly matched for the load and then geared to run slightly above the engine's maximum torque speed. For most of the engines we use in RVs, that's about 2,500 rpm.

Judging from what I've seen lately, a lot of new truck buyers aren't getting that engine speed. The result is, they aren't getting the pulling power and economy they should. If you have selected a new truck recently and based your choice of gear ratios on what you had before, you may be sorry.

ARE YOU LOSING POWER?

Until recently, most light trucks used LT235/75-15

tires. With 3.70-1 gears, that gave about 2,450 rpm. That's not too bad. If your engine was right for the load, you were probably satisfied with that choice. So, when it came time for a new truck, you stayed loyal to your brand and ordered the same engine and gear ratio. But this time the truck came with LT235/85-16 tires. Now your engine is turning only about 2,200 rpm. Everything is nice and quiet, but the new truck doesn't have the power the old one had. Is there something wrong with the engine? Nope, it's the tires.

Those new tires are about three inches taller than the old ones. They make a lot fewer turns per mile and should wear longer, but the effect on overall gearing is more than expected. To get the same engine speed you had with the old truck and 3.70 gearing, you now need 4.11 gearing. Most of you didn't get it.

Are there any advantages to the new, larger tires? Well, you get about 1.5 inches more clearance under the differential, and you should get a bit longer wear. You may get a bit better fuel mileage when you aren't pulling a load. But fuel mileage when pulling will likely go down a bit. Here's why.

Because of the effective gear reduction (numerically), your engine is working harder to do the same job. Most induction systems, carburetors or injectors, are programmed to let the engine burn a richer mixture when it has to work hard. That's necessary to keep the valves and piston heads from getting too hot and burning. If you had vacuum gauges on both vehicles, you would observe that the new one is running lower vacuum than the older one under the same conditions. Low vacuum indicates a harder working engine.

What can you do about it? Not much.

You might swap to smaller tires on the same wheels, but that wouldn't gain very much, and you would lose carrying capacity. If you're really unhappy, you might try and find a set of 15-inch wheels and go back to LT235/75-15 tires. That's about all you can do other than changing the gears. With the price of new tires and wheels, changing gears with a used set from the salvage yard might be the best bet. Of course, if you haven't yet ordered the new truck, you can make sure you get the right gearing.

Chapter 25

Tools and Things You Need For Your RV

It isn't true that we RVers are first cousins to packrats. It's just that we need some goodies in our homes on wheels if we are going to find using them comfortable. Little things like ...

Well, tools, for example. When you live in something as mechanical as an RV, there are occasional needs to fix or change something. Life is a lot more pleasant when the right tool is handy. Not all RVers are or want to be shade tree mechanics. But most seem to get pleasure out of doing a portion of their own maintenance work. The degree of involvement will determine which tools you need.

I suggest a set of combination end wrenches sized from three-eights inch up to one inch. One end is open and the other end is hex head. As with all tools, it doesn't pay to buy cheap ones. Good ones cost only a little more and last much longer. Sears has good hand tools at reasonable prices.

You will also need a spark plug wrench. I like the kind that has a flexible joint as part of the socket. You will need a straight extension and ratchet handle to fit. While you're at it, get a spark plug gapping tool.

An adjustable wrench about 10 inches long is always handy. When you use it, be sure to adjust the opening to a snug fit.

A pair of cotton gloves and an old shirt and pants will help to keep you and your other clothes clean.

HALF A DOZEN SCREWDRIVERS

Get a half dozen screwdrivers. You will need straight blades in about three sizes from small to large. Also get one stubby with a medium size blade. Get a couple of Phillips head drivers, medium and large. Plastic handles are good.

Buy a good tire gauge and treat it with respect. Most gauges that you find on air hoses are inaccurate. Dial gauges are the ones usually recommended but I use the pencil type. Check your tire pressures when they are cool. An hour's driving on a hot day will increase pressures by five pounds or more. That's okay. Never lower the pressure of a warm tire. Start with the recommended cold pressure for your load and let them build up as you drive.

You will need a lug wrench to fit all your wheels. You can get the kind that looks like a big cross and has four different sizes. They are good, but they do take up space. I like to use a socket with a short extension and a good handle about 15 inches long.

A pipe wrench about 18 inches long will sooner or later be worth its weight in gold. A machinist's hammer will also be useful.

A BOX FOR THE TOOLS

With all of those tools, you will need a toolbox. Buy one about twice as large as you think you will need. Tools have a habit of breeding when you put them together, and they soon outgrow the space you provide. I've got several small boxes to prove it. My toolbox is about 18 inches long with two pullout drawers and a tray under the lid. Even with that, I have another large box that usually stays in the garage.

No one likes to think about flat tires, but they do happen, especially if you don't have a good jack. Get a hydraulic jack with enough power to lift half your RV or three tons, whichever is greater. To keep that jack from disappearing into the soft earth, carry an assortment of wood blocks. One should be two inches thick and about 8 X 10 inches. Also get a piece of plywood or paneling about 18 inches square for a kneeling pad to keep you out of the dirt.

That wheel that came with your trailer and fits on the jack post probably has some useful purpose. When you find out what it is, let me know. Better than the wheel when you park is a block of wood eight inches square and four inches thick. I've seen adjustable metal "blocks" that look good, too.

LEVELS AND BLOCKS

A leveling block to drive a wheel up on is essential for leveling your RV. I've cut four pieces of 2 X 6 with an angle on one end of each. They are 60 inches, 54 inches, 48 inches and 42 inches long. Stack them to furnish the height needed.

How can you tell how much is needed? It used to be trial and error. Not now. I found a level that mounts on the front of the trailer where I can see it in the mirror. It's marked off so that each mark indicates about one inch of tilt. Back into place, read the marks, pull forward. Place the required number of boards in place, and back up until you're level. The level also has a small level for reading the fore and aft tilt.

Motorhomes will use two small levels mounted next to the driver. They will also need more than one set of leveling blocks.

Parking chocks placed on the downhill side of your wheels when you park can give peace of mind. I've parked in spots where having the rig roll would have been disastrous. Make your own chocks or buy a set made of aluminum and use them.

Parking stands are used to make your RV steady when parked. Don't use them to try and level the rig. That puts too much strain on the frame. Parking stands usually come in a set of four. I seldom use more than two placed under the rear of the trailer.

MISCELLANEOUS GEAR

You will want to take a few spare cans of oil with you. Also carry a spare can of transmission fluid and a can of brake fluid. A plastic box is handy to hold these.

Many RVers install and use a CB radio. These are handy to keep contact with other travelers or to call for emergency help. Once, when the small motorcycle I was carrying on the back of the trailer came loose from inadequate mounts, I was very glad a trucker called on the CB to let me know. Amateur radio operators know that they have a better idea. Talk with one and find out what it is.

Maps and campground guides are indispensable. Clear up the clutter by keeping them in a small box cut to fit under the seat or some other convenient location. The same box can contain a package of wipes, those moist tissues that are so handy for cleaning up after a sandwich or fried chicken lunch. Keep small plastic trash bags there, too.

Shock cords, or bungees, are useful in many ways. Carry a half dozen of assorted lengths. A piece of three-eighths-inch polyethylene rope about 50 feet long will save your day sometime. I hope you never need a tow chain or tow strap, but if you do you won't have the chance to walk across the street and buy one. A dependable rule is that emergencies never occur in convenient places. Don't get a tow cable. They cause more trouble than they are worth.

Another item I hope you never need is a set of emergency triangles -- those little reflective devices you set out to warn other drivers that you are stranded. If you drive at night, add a couple of flares.

Go to the nearest surplus store and buy an entrenching tool. It's a small, folding shovel that every RVer should have. The next time you have a low tire while sitting on top of a mountain, you'll wish you had a tire pump. Get one before you go up the mountain. Some of the electric ones are good but, old-fashioned boy that I am, I like the hand pump.

A gallon water container will come in handy when your radiator decides things have been going too smoothly. It can fit in that box that's holding your cans of oil. A set of heavy-duty jumper cables will be very useful on that morning when either you or your RV end up with a dead battery. Your auxiliary battery may be all you need for a start, but without the jump cords, you're dead in the water. Get #4 copper wire. Smaller wire or aluminum won't carry enough current.

Chapter 26

Towing Tips

Not a month goes by that I don't receive several letters from first-time RVers asking for help. Most of them have just bought a trailer that their dealer told them could be towed by the family car or truck. Then the owners found out that they couldn't. Can I help them?

I really feel for new RVers. It's an intriguing world of adventure and fun. There is no better way to enjoy the United States and Canada than with an RV. And I think a trailer is the most adaptable RV.

But, too many times the first choice of trailer and tow vehicle is wrong and the owner becomes unhappy and decides to quit. That's too bad. Sometimes the problem can be corrected at a relatively minor expense. Other times it can't. But the problem can always be avoided by careful appraisal and selection of the combination of trailer, tow vehicle and associated hitch.

In order to tow any trailer with comfort and safety, the tow vehicle must have sufficient engine power to handle the load, gearing that permits the engine to do its job, a hitch that eliminates sway, and comfortable passenger space. With today's smaller cars and the emphasis on fuel economy, there are no more than a half dozen cars built that can adequately tow a trailer weighing 4,000 pounds. I'm aware that the manufacturers of these half dozen cars rate them to tow 5,000 lbs. The problem is that even though the engines might be willing, the gearing is wrong.

CHOOSE THE RIGHT TOW VEHICLE

Another problem with many recent cars is the lack of a frame to attach a hitch. Serious damage has been done to some cars when their owners insisted that a too-heavy trailer and hitch be attached. If you must tow with a car, either get one from the early '70s or one of the recent models with a V-8 engine. Order it with the highest numerical rear axle ratio available and stick with a trailer weighing no more than 4,000 pounds when loaded.

If cars can't do the job of towing a travel trailer safely, that still leaves some very inviting choices. Standard-size vans, utility vehicles and the Suburban by Chevrolet and GMC make excellent tow vehicles while offering passenger comfort on a par with the best automobiles. For couples with no need for more than two passengers, extended-cab pickups are an excellent choice. They offer a high degree of traveling comfort and adequate space in the rear seat for the things travelers like to have handy. Even though they look large and a trifle ungainly, I've found that my Ford Supercab turns in less space than the vans I formerly used.

The major advantage of standard-size vans, utility vehicles and pickups is that they offer large engines and adequate gearing to move heavy loads easily. That can't be overemphasized. A car may seem to give tremendous performance with its normal passenger load. But when you hang an additional 5,000 pounds behind it, it goes to sleep.

It is unreasonable to ask a car to tow double or more the weight it was designed to handle. Trucks and vans have the engines and gearing to move a load. With the proper choice of engine and gearing, these vehicles can give good towing performance with trailers weighing 12,000 pounds or more.

GEAR RATIO IS CRITICAL

With fuel prices rising and the EPA emphasizing fuel economy, many owners are asking for a combination-use vehicle. "I need something to tow my 6,000-pound trailer for maybe 30% of the time. The rest of the driving is to and from work and to the store. I need fuel economy," the plaint goes.

Suppose for a moment that you bought a van with a small V-8 engine and gearing around 3.25-1 so that you could get good solo mileage and still tow your 5,000-pound trailer. There are a lot of people doing just that. The salesman will assure you that everything will be all right. Then, further suppose that on your next vacation, you're trying to enjoy the mountains when you suddenly realize that your engine has slowed down, road speed has dropped to a crawl and then the engine just stops. As you back down the mountain looking for a place to turn around, the kids are crying and your wife is making sharp comments. Do you suppose you will be having good thoughts about your great solo mileage?

It doesn't happen that way? Yes, it does. I've personally known one driver, a relative, who backed a mile and a half knowing that if he made one mistake in keeping things straight, he didn't have the power to move forward to correct the error. Another reader wrote that he had backed five miles, and another swears he backed 10 miles. He probably didn't, but I'm sure it seemed like 10 miles.

There is one rule. If you're going to tow a load, make absolutely certain that you have the power and gearing to do it right. Power and gear for the tow; let the solo mileage take care of itself. What you save in high solo mileage is peanuts compared with what you lose in towing performance.

Also, when solo mileage is emphasized, engine and transmission life are shortened during towing. The engine and transmission work harder, temperatures rise, there is little reserve power for hills and passing, and towing mileage is reduced.

FOLLOW THESE GUIDELINES

So, how do you know what is correct power and gearing? All the factories have their towing guides that should help, but they don't. The emphasis is too much on solo mileage to meet EPA mileage requirements. You will have to make the judgments.

Here are some rules of thumb. The various engines in the 3.8-liter to 4.3-liter class are good for a maximum trailer weight of about 4,000 pounds when used in the small vans and small utility vehicles with gear ratios of around 3.73-1. The 5.0-liter engines increase capacity to perhaps 5,500 pounds in standard vans, utility vehicles and pickups. Gearing should range from 3.55-1 for 4,000 pounds to 4.10-1 for 5,500 pounds when the vehicle is fitted with 15-inch tires. Moving to 5.7-liter engines gives another 1,000 pounds of capacity using 3.55-1 gear ratios for 4,500 pounds of trailer and up to 4.10-1 gearing for 6,500 pounds with 15-inch tires. With 16-inch tires, start the gearing at 3.73-1. Heavier trailers require the largest engines available with gear ratios from 4.10-1 to 4.56-1.

Why all the discussion about gearing and tires? What does tire size have to do with it?

The power an engine can produce is determined in large part by the speed it runs -- its revolutions per minute (RPM). Up to its maximum rated speed, the faster an engine runs the more power it can produce. If the tire size and gears are such that engine speed is kept low, the engine can't develop the power for which it was rated. As an example, the Ford 5.8-liter EFI engine is rated at 210 horsepower at 3800 rpm. In a truck fitted with 3.55 gearing and 235/85-16 tires, the engine turns about 2450 rpm at 60 miles per hour. With that gearing and tire size, the engine can develop no more than 145 horsepower to pull your trailer up the mountain. With the same size tires and 4.10 gearing it turns about 2800 rpm at 60 mph and can develop as much as 170 horsepower. The extra 25 horses can be important.

TIRE SIZE IS IMPORTANT TOO

Tire size is part of the overall gear ratio and must be factored in. Most of our gasoline engines work best and produce their best overall economy when geared to tow at 2600 to 2900 rpm. For heavier trailers within an engine's weight range, use gearing to produce higher engine speeds. Then buy a transmission with an overdrive for solo driving and good fuel mileage. But forget about towing in overdrive. The overdrive gear in conventional automatics is made too small to handle the load even if the engine could produce the power.

For those of you who own a vehicle that you want to adapt for towing, use the same information working backward to select the size trailer you can tow comfortably. Resist the urge to stretch the vehicle's capability. If you find yourself with one of today's miracle vehicles with a moderate size engine that offers towing possibilities but has a gear ratio of 3.42 or less, consider changing the gears to something more suitable. The cost will run from $350 to near $900 depending upon make and model. That's hefty money but still cheaper than repairing a transmission or swapping for a newer and larger vehicle.

Every tow vehicle needs a hitch if it's going to pull a trailer. Travel trailers must be used with hitches that have equalizing bars to help control the tongue weight. The bars should be balanced to the load. Bars that are too stiff give an uncomfortable ride and produce stresses that break equipment. Be sure the hitch is properly installed by someone who knows what he is doing.

With most hitches, there is always the possibility of induced sway between the tow vehicle and trailer by cross winds, passing trucks or corrective movements of steering. Some of the sway can be controlled by using sway bars that tend to resist the yawing action. There is one hitch, the Pullrite, that eliminates sway entirely by moving the pivot between tow vehicle and trailer to just behind the tow vehicle's rear axle. The combination can't sway.

COOLERS, BRAKES AND MIRRORS

Any tow vehicle with an automatic transmission -- the best choice for most drivers -- must have an auxiliary transmission cooler. When moving a heavy load, automatics produce a lot of heat. If the heat is not dissipated, the transmission fluid oxidizes and becomes abrasive. A ruined transmission is expensive to repair.

Play it safe by installing an auxiliary cooler rated for at least 150% of the gross combined weight of the tow vehicle and trailer. Very few of the auxiliary coolers installed by the manufacturers are large enough for more than small trailers.

Any travel trailer needs brakes of its own. Nearly all use electric brakes powered by the tow vehicle's battery and actuated by pressure on the tow vehicle brakes. Until recently, nearly all used a controller that tapped into the tow vehicle's hydraulic brake lines. Recent changes by the manufacturers have nearly eliminated this possibility. Brake controllers now use electronic means of measuring the braking action of the tow vehicle and actuating the trailer brakes accordingly. The action isn't quite as smooth, but the controllers work. Get the best you can afford.

Finally, a tow vehicle needs large mirrors so that the driver can see down the sides of the trailer when driving. Since few drivers want the large mirrors in place permanently unless they do a lot of towing, some kind of temporary mirror is best. There are clip-on mirrors that attach to the front fenders or the front doors. The ones on the fenders are easy to see but difficult to see out of. That is, the image they produce is so narrow that it is almost useless. Get the type that clip on the doors.

There you have it. Sounds like a lot doesn't it? I agree, but it's worth doing right. RVing with a properly balanced tow vehicle and trailer offers a level of freedom and relaxation that is difficult to match. Your home is literally wherever you park it. Thousands of campgrounds in some of the most beautiful mountains or deserts you can imagine await you. Fortunately, they don't build motels there. Take your own little apartment on wheels. Take your trailer.

If you have questions about the suitability of your tow vehicle and trailer combination, write to me in care of Cottage Publications, 24396 Pleasant View Dr., Elkhart, IN 46517. Enclose a stamped, self-addressed envelope for an answer.

Chapter 27

Tow Vehicle: Selecting One Best For Your Use

With the exception of writing the check, selecting and buying a new tow vehicle is a real pleasure. I enjoy sitting down with weight charts and horsepower, torque and fuel-use curves and figuring out the best combination for my travels. I admit that those bits of information can be intimidating at first, but I'll take the mystery out of it for you.

In selecting the best tow vehicle for your use, there are several factors that have to be considered. Among the most obvious are weight of the combined vehicles, horsepower, engine torque, wheelbase, gearing and tire size. Let's take a look at each factor and see the implications for towing. We will start with wheelbase.

Wheelbase is not too important until you start maneuvering, especially backing into a campsite. Then it becomes critical. Wheelbase also effects ride comfort and passenger capacity of the tow vehicle. The longer the wheelbase, the better the ride. But the longer the wheelbase, the more difficult controlled backing becomes. Full-size vans, with their wheelbase running up to 138 inches, make excellent tow vehicles for families needing the passenger space and pulling trailers over 22 feet. But backing a shorter trailer with a tow vehicle with a 138-inch wheelbase can be a problem.

The problem is less with a Reese-type hitch than with a PullRite. For 25 years, I used Reese-type hitches on all sorts of tow vehicles. They have an advantage in backing up because the pivot point is from three to five or more feet behind the rear axle. Turning the front end of the tow vehicle to make a backing turn swings the front of the trailer to help make the turn. Just what you want.

LEVERAGE BECOMES SWAY

But, that same leverage works against you when moving down the road. Any force acting on the trailer -- wind, bumps or fast-moving trucks -- tends to steer the tow vehicle. We call it sway and attempt to control it with sway bars.

The PullRite hitch works differently. The pivot point is only a few inches behind the tow vehicle axle. There is no sway. But there also is no swing of the rear of the tow vehicle to help turn the trailer. I like the PullRite hitch. But after pulling a 24-foot trailer several thousand miles with a full-size Ford van, I realized that a tow vehicle with a shorter wheelbase would offer greater maneuverability. I think about 116-inch to 120-inch wheelbase would be great. I know from having used vehicles in that range in the past that the ride will still be satisfactory, and maneuverability will be improved. Vehicles that size can carry up to five people comfortably, but if you need greater passenger capacity, you may have to go to a slightly longer wheelbase.

Short-wheelbase vehicles such as the Blazer and Bronco work fine with the PullRite hitch. They don't work quite so well with Reese-type hitches and trailers over 20 feet in length. They give great maneuverability, but the short wheelbase doesn't have enough leverage to work against the sway of longer trailers.

CARRYING ABILITY VS RIDE

Weight-carrying capacity of the tow vehicle is usually not important unless you're pulling a fifth-wheel trailer. Standard travel trailers should always be used with a weight-distributing hitch. The resulting weight on the rear of the tow vehicle is seldom enough to cause a problem so long as tires are large enough. More about that later. One important factor to keep in mind is that excess weight-carrying capacity gives an unnecessarily rough ride when the trailer is not attached. Most so-called half-ton vehicles are adequate for towing most travel trailers. Fifth wheelers will usually need more.

Weight-moving capacity is an important factor, however. That brings us to engine and gear selection. We'll take the engine first.

It's mistake to ask the tow vehicle salesman for help. Long experience has shown me that the car or truck salesman who knows the vehicle he is selling is a rare bird. Yes, he knows the popular accessories and he knows the price. Beyond that he is lost. And no wonder. His job is largely dealing with customers who are rarely interested in more than those factors. Most customers buy vehicles already on the lot.

But you are different. You want a vehicle that is not only comfortable, but also one that will do an unusual job: move itself and another large load with relative ease and reasonable economy. That takes careful selection. All manufacturers of the types of vehicles you're likely to consider publish recommendations for towing. Again, there are problems. Government regulations for the past several years have stressed fuel economy. The result is that manufacturers' recommendations reflect a bias toward economy when the vehicle is not under heavy load. The towing performance suffers.

WEIGHT/HORSEPOWER RATIO

So, what to do? First, decide what kind of performance you must have. That boils down to a weight/horsepower ratio and a consideration of the towing terrain. With any engine, there are two factors that must be considered -- horsepower and torque. Horsepower is the force that accelerates your vehicle and climbs the hills. Torque is the force that moves you down the road. It takes a lot of horsepower to give reasonable acceleration or take you over that mountain pass at a decent speed. It takes far less horsepower to move you down the road once you have reached cruising speed.

Let's look at required horsepower. Truckers work with pounds of weight per horsepower ratios as high as 300:1. That is, they may have only one horsepower for every 300 pounds they are moving. But if you have followed a truck trying to accelerate on an entrance ramp or climb a steep hill after it has lost its momentum, you know that you wouldn't be satisfied with that kind of performance.

How does that compare with what you're used to? Many of our cars today operate at ratios of around 30:1. Obviously, that gives much better acceleration and hill-climbing performance. With proper gearing, high ratios give better economy but poorer acceleration than low ratios. Truckers are willing to accept high load/horsepower ratios for the improved fuel mileage they get.

But most RVers are not truck drivers. We are accustomed to punching the pedal to the floor and having things happen now, not tomorrow. We should remember we can't have that kind of performance when moving heavy loads. Our 9,000 pounds or more don't begin to reach the levels of the truckers, but we do need to adopt an attitude that accepts less performance than we get with a lightly loaded car.

I've found that most RVers will be satisfied with ratios between 50 and 100:1, depending upon the terrain.

Good performance in the mountains will be easier with 50:1. Flat lands can be handled at 100:1. But remember that the same highway that runs through the flatlands also runs through mountains. Most trailerists eventually find themselves looking at the point where the land meets the sky.

THE RIGHT SIZE ENGINE

To select the right size engine, just determine your gross combined vehicle weight and divide by the number you have decided will give you the performance you want. If fuel economy is important to you, you'll lean closer to the 100. As a caution, remember Farlow's First Rule: The horsepower you don't buy will be exactly the amount needed to get over that next mountain pass.

Recent action by the Environmental Protection Agency has posed another factor you might wish to consider in selecting your engine. Regulations released in 1985 called for the total phase-out of lead in gasoline by January 1, 1988. Just before that date, the EPA announced that it would postpone final phase-out for an indefinite time. (The issue has become more complicated because most oil companies are eliminating leaded fuel. Market demand has reached the point that leaded fuel is no longer economical for them to produce.)

Research that the EPA released in 1987 showed clearly that use of unleaded fuel was very harmful to engines operating under heavy-duty conditions, the exact conditions RVs face. The continuing problem is that all gasoline-powered vehicles we are likely to select -- who among us is going to buy a five-ton truck? -- are equipped with catalytic converters and require unleaded fuel. I would be very hesitant to invest in a new, expensive gasoline engine today. Diesel is one answer but, like most choices, it also presents some problems.

The next consideration is gearing and tire size. The two go together because tire size effects overall gearing. What you want is the gearing that will let your engine operate at its most economical speed when you are at cruising speed. That's why you need to know your engine's torque curve. Your dealer can find it for you if he will. Don't accept his memory. See the numbers for yourself. Every engine manufacturer publishes charts that show the information you need.

THE TORQUE DIFFERENCE

Most engines that you will be interested in develop maximum torque somewhere between 2,400 and 2,800 revolutions per minute (rpm). With few exceptions, engines have their lowest fuel consumption rates at speeds slightly above maximum torque speed. That is the speed at which they give the best economy. That's the speed you want the engine to run when you are at cruising speed. How do you get it? The information in the accompanying article shows you how.

Since tow vehicles usually get far more use in solo running than they do pulling, you may want to consider one more factor. In following the above suggestions, you will get a vehicle that is right for towing but is over-powered and over-geared for running solo. If that bothers you, you might want to get an aftermarket overdrive unit.

I have used a Gear Vendors unit with a gear ratio of .77. That provides 23% overdrive when running solo. It also provides six forward speeds. Five of them can be used for towing according to the conditions. I've used them all.

Finally, we get to transmissions. Nearly every manufacturer recommends or requires an automatic transmission as part of its towing package. I suspect the reasons have more to do with today's drivers than anything else. Very few drivers have much experience with heavy loads and stick shifts. The result is short life for clutches. Manufacturers don't like to deal with those kinds of complaints. It's easier for them to say, "Get an automatic."

MANUAL OR AUTOMATIC SHIFT?

I used to use stick shifts for all my tow vehicles. They give better engine braking on downgrades and slightly better fuel mileage. But I never liked them for close maneuvering. The last several years, I've used automatics and learned to like them. With adequate cooling, they are at least as durable as a stick shift. There is also the ease with which you make manual shifts and never give a thought to the possibility of missing a shift.

Manual shifting an automatic is important. When climbing, if you wait for the transmission to downshift, you've waited too long. The engine has slowed to the point that it is below good pulling speed, and your carburetor is into the enrichment zone. Fuel economy has long since departed, and your engine is beginning to get too warm. Don't be afraid to downshift manually and keep those engine revolutions up to where it is working easily.

Also be sure to add an auxiliary transmission cooler for that automatic. If your dealer says the one that comes with the rig is enough, just smile. Then buy one that is amply large for the combined weight of trailer and tow vehicle. Cooler manufacturers rate their products for a maximum combined vehicle weight. I prefer to select one for 150% to 200% of the combined weight. The additional cost is about five dollars. You'll be glad you spent it. Be sure, too, that you get the largest radiator you can when you order the tow vehicle. Long mountain climbs on hot summer days generate lots of heat. Heat is an engine's enemy. Defeat it!

Now get those charts and brochures and build yourself a dream tow vehicle. That's the part of selecting a tow vehicle that is pure pleasure. The payoff comes when you see the highway begin to go up and up and you know that you've got the little tow vehicle that could. If you have questions about your selection I'll try to help. Write me in care of Cottage Publications, 24396 Pleasant View Dr., Elkhart, IN 46517. Include a business-size self-addressed stamped envelope.

Chapter 28

Truckers Talk About Mileage

How would you like to double the fuel economy of your RV rig? Me, too. Until lately, I thought it wasn't possible. Now I'm not so sure.

Years ago. I drove a truck for a living, and I've kept a passing interest in trucks over the years. One thing that always bothered me was that the mileage I was getting on my RV wasn't much better than those trucks were getting. Look at it this way: If an 80,000-pound 18-wheeler can get 5 to 6 miles per gallon, it seems to me that a 9,000-pound trailer and truck combination ought to be getting better than its 10.5 mpg.

Then I happened to pick up a copy of "TRUCKS," and one of the articles tossed a huge serving of salt on my wounds. Virgil Pound, product integrity manager for Peterbilt Motors Company, the manufacturer of some of those big rigs, said, "The industry is not too far from the time when 80,000-pound Class 8 rigs will consistently be turning in fuel economy figures of 10 mpg or better." That hurt. It could be just talk, but it still hurt.

What hurt even more was another article I recently read in another magazine reporting that Roger Penske, the race car owner-driver, has modified a big 18-wheeler used to transport his race cars and equipment so that the rig is getting an incredible 8.3 mpg. That was a better than 50% improvement over the unmodified rig he was previously using.

It's true that his load of race cars and equipment probably is somewhat less than 80,000 pounds, but you can bet your next year's fuel budget that it is a whole lot more than our 9,000 pounds. What's going on here, anyway? I had to find out.

BASIS OF THE CLAIMS

I started by contacting Peterbilt Motors and asked Mr. Pound what he was basing his claims of a soon-to-be 10 mpg on. What I got back was a report on some research done by Peterbilt to find out where the power (fuel) was going and what could be done about it. It was interesting material, and most of it can be translated to our RVs.

Well over half of the energy in the fuel burned is totally lost, producing no power for us at all. Those losses go out the exhaust pipe in the form of combustion losses and into heat that is dissipated through the surface of the engine and the radiator. There isn't much that we can do about these losses. They are a part of the process of converting fuel energy into engine power. There are some possibilities, though.

Aircraft designers have found that they can increase the efficiency of airplanes dramatically by paying careful attention to engine cooling capacity. Most older aircraft were overcooled. The result was wasted fuel and decreased speed. Sizing the cooling air intake to supply only what was needed gave an increase in fuel efficiency and speed.

It has occurred to me that RV manufacturers have given little attention to the size of the air passages leading to our radiators. They seem to just put a big opening out there and assume it will work. The result is likely to be a lot more air than necessary churning around that engine. Remember, air that is being seriously disrupted in its flow means energy lost. An RVer might well find that a bit of mileage could be picked up by careful attention to the size of his radiator grill opening.

ROLLING RESISTENCE

But there is a lot more. Of the power that is actually generated by the engine and available for work, approximately 40% is used to overcome rolling resistance. The main factors here are weight, tire and tire-related resistance, and road speed. Up to 10% improvement can be realized by careful attention to these factors. Let's look at them one at a time.

We all know that the more weight we carry around, the more energy it takes to move that weight. When was the last time you cleaned out the debris (valuable objects) collected from your RV trips? You will be surprised at the amount of weight that can be removed by getting rid of those non-essentials.

There is also the question of how much water you need to carry. If your trip is going to terminate for the night at a site that has water hook-ups or a place to fill the tank, why carry 40 gallons of water for 400 miles? That 40 gallons weighs 320 lbs and takes energy to move. If your RV weighs 9,000 pounds, those 40 gallons of water mean a savings of 3.6%. Significant? I think so.

You can probably think of other ways to lower the weight of your rig. One way you may not have thought of is to write a letter, several letters. RV manufacturers are aware that weight reduction means fuel economy. They may not be aware that we know it and are willing to look for it. Remind them -- frequently -- that we want fuel economy in our rigs and then look for it. When shopping new rigs. ask about the weight. Make pointed comments to the salesperson about the weight being too high. If enough of us were to become weight conscious in our shopping and tell manufacturers what we are looking for, we could get lighter weight and more efficient RVs.

TIRE-RELATED ENERGY LOSS

The second factor in rolling resistance is tire-related. Let's start with the tires you presently have. We all know that tires running at low pressure flex more than if they are at a higher pressure. That flexing takes energy and costs you fuel as well as tire life. For every 5% a tire is underinflated, the fuel consumption increases by 1%. If your tires are supposed to be inflated to 45 pounds but you are running at 43 pounds, you are losing nearly 1% in fuel mileage. Not much but it all adds up.

The best rule is to inflate to a pressure adequate to carry your load but stay within the limits of your tire size. I like to run at near the upper inflation limit recommended by the tire manufacturer.

When it comes time to buy replacement tires, you have other mileage considerations. Bias-ply tires may cost less than radial-ply tires, but they cost more in terms of fuel. All tires flex as they roll down the road. The design of radials lets them flex more easily, using less energy. An additional advantage of radials is that they usually last longer and can often be recapped for additional economy. Remember, though, that the wheels on some older RVs can't handle radials. Look for an "R" or the word "radial" stamped on the wheel.

The tread design on your new tires is important, too. Rib tread designs roll easier than block treads or all-weather treads. The tradeoff is traction. Rib treads don't give quite as much traction as all-weather treads. Look for a compromise.

RECONSIDER REAR DUALS

If you are buying a new rig or have an older one that you are going to keep for a while, consider the question of rear duals. Duals not only increase the rolling resistance when compared with wide-base singles, but they also increase the wind resistance and they cost more. With newer suspension systems available, I have serious doubts about the need for duals for many installations. Yes, there are some RVs that need duals for weight carrying capacity. But many of these could use good singles and experience a savings in fuel.

The next factor in rolling resistance is one that some of us don't want to hear. Driving fast uses more fuel. One rule of thumb is that each mph over 55 mph increases fuel requirements by 1.5 to 2.5%. That means driving 60 instead of 55 mph may be costing you over 1 mpg if you are now getting 9 mpg.

Another series of factors in the mileage marathon are those associated with air drag and aerodynamics. Automobile manufacturers have become more aware of aerodynamics. We are beginning to see references in advertising material to "coefficient of drag." Coefficient of drag is simply the factor that measures the ability of the vehicle to push the air out of its path. The less the air is disturbed, the less energy and fuel is required. The auto manufacturers have become interested in good coefficient of drag factors because of the government's insistence on better mileage figures.

BETTER AERODYNAMICS

We have tended to accept that RVs are inherently inefficient at moving through the air and that there is nothing we can do about it. Truckers used to feel that way, too. With the increases in fuel cost of the last several years, lots of people are taking a second look. Peterbilt has found that aerodynamic improvements can give fuel savings of 5 to 11%. Even 5% can be significant in the total savings picture.

Let's look at some factors involved in aerodynamics and ways we can improve them.

The frontal area of your rig is one factor that is very important in aerodynamics. Frontal area is simply the width multiplied by the height. Not much you do about that is there? Wrong! If you are towing a trailer, there is a lot you can do to reduce the effective frontal area. It is highly probable that you are pushing the air out of the way more than once.

Let's start with a worst case, one that is very common. You are towing a trailer with a car. As you drive down the road, the car pushes the air aside and up and over itself. The air tends to flow over the top of the car and down over the trunk and rear of the car. There it hits the front of the trailer. The car hasn't done a thing to improve the flow of air over the trailer. If your car has a frontal area of 30 square feet and your trailer has a frontal area of 72 square feet, you are working with a total effective frontal area of 102 square feet. Wouldn't it be nice if you could push that air out of the way only once instead of twice and get an effective frontal area more nearly equal to that of the trailer? Well, you can.

TRY A WIND DEFLECTOR

You've seen those big wind deflectors on top of the cabs of trucks. Some RVers are putting them on their tow vehicles. Maybe you've wondered whether they work. They do -- sometimes. Peterbilt found them effective, but they have to be big enough and properly placed or they don't help. As Tom Clayton reported in the May 1986 "Trailer Life," wind deflectors have to be much larger than most people think if they are going to work. The reasons are easy to understand if we just think about it.

What we want to do is gently push the air from one location to another and make sure that it goes where we want. The deflector should be large enough in height to move the air from the top of the tow vehicle to the top of the trailer and wide enough to move it to the sides of the trailer. Anything less means we are going to dump that air against a solid, vertical surface and that means increased drag.

The deflector must also be placed close enough to the trailer that the air has little chance to flow downward instead of up and over the trailer. That's almost impossible to do when towing with a car. A station wagon, pickup with a topper, or a van makes it easier. A pickup without a topper is as bad a case as a car.

If the front of your trailer has a gentle slope to the rear near the roof line, you may be able to get by with a deflector that is somewhat lower in height by setting the angle of the deflector to blend with the slope of the trailer front.

SHAPE NOT SO IMPORTANT

One interesting thing found in the Peterbilt study is that the shape of the front of the vehicle is not as important as we thought. Peterbilt discovered there was little difference in fuel required with a conventional tractor versus a cabover. At the speeds that we drive, the dominant factor is effective frontal area.

Peterbilt also found that fairings from the sides of the tractor running back as near as possible to the front of the trailer were helpful in improving mileage. There doesn't seem to be a lot that we can do in this area. I can hardly imagine anyone installing such fairings to the sides of his tow vehicle, but perhaps some ingenious owner will find a way.

Rounded corners where sides and roof meet are also effective in producing a better coefficient of drag. While you aren't likely to take a saw to your present trailer to round those edges, you might want to consider this factor when shopping for a new rig. Similarly, look for a rig that has a downward slope to the roof toward the rear. The ideal shape would be a teardrop, but no manufacturer is going to go to that extreme. But any improvement in this direction will help.

The worst aerodynamic cases are the bunkhouse arrangements that produce an enlarged vertical cross-section at the rear. The result is lots of turbulence as the air comes off the roof and sides. The greater the turbulence, the greater the power required. I haven't seen anyone try it, but I'm quite sure that a horizontal deflector across the rear roof line turning the air flow down would help. Some station wagons have similar deflectors to improve the air flow and help keep the rear window clean.

NIX TO STORAGE PODS

Shape and placement of external storage pods is another area that needs to get more careful consideration. Lots of us seem to need more storage than is available inside our RVs. Storage pods, those big containers that go on top of trailers and motorhomes, are a popular solution to the problem. But look at their shape. The fronts are typically rounded from a horizontal center line so that air is forced to go both over the top and down to the bottom of the pod.

What happens to the air that goes toward the bottom? It gets caught between the pod and the RV roof and becomes turbulent, more power wasted. A better design would taper up from a bottom line as near the roof as possible. The result would be less turbulence and less wasted power.

Placement, too is important. We have all seen large, rectangular pods mounted across the RV. That increases the frontal area and means wasted power pushing the air out of the way. Better positioning would place the narrow dimension across the RV. On RVs that have a break in the roof line with the height becoming less toward the rear, the best position of the pod would have the front of the pod as near as possible to that break. Then air coming off the high portion of the roof would tend to flow directly over the top of the pod rather than move down to the roof and then be forced up and over the pod. If more than one pod is needed, they should be placed in line and as closely together as possible. One large pod would be more aerodynamically efficient than two small ones.

Those big, West Coast-style mirrors are a negative factor in aerodynamics, too. I know, they look macho. But they do have lots of drawbacks. For one thing, they cover up a lot of the view. Driving is always safer when the view is open. They also make a lot of wind-noise. That means they are disrupting the airflow and costing fuel. Not a lot, I agree. But when we're after top fuel efficiency, we have to look for the small things. After trying the West Coast-style mirrors, I found that I was happier with low-mounted swingaway mirrors such as Ford and others have. They are out of the way visually, and they don't make as much noise -- less fuel wasted and a more comfortable ride.

HOLD DOWN YOUR SPEED

Speed is another factor in aerodynamics. We really have to look at total air speed. That means road speed plus wind speed. If we are traveling at 55 mph into a headwind of 20 mph, our air speed is 75 mph. Since the effect of wind speed is cubed in figuring power required, this means that maintaining a road speed of 55 into that 20 mph headwind requires 2.5 times as much power. You may not be able to reduce the headwind, but you can reduce your road speed and save fuel.

Reduction of powertrain losses offer the potential of 2% to 10% fuel savings. Powertrain losses result from friction and parasitic losses in such areas as the engine (intake and exhaust losses), transmission, axles, and such accessories as cooling fan, alternator, air conditioner and power steering. Most of these are essential to either our or our RV's comfort. But they all offer the possibility of savings.

One example is the cooling fan. On some of the large engines we use, the cooling fan may use as much as 25 horsepower when running. But 95% of the time, the forward motion of the RV furnishes sufficient cooling air. Only 5% of the time is the fan needed. A fan with a temperature-actuated clutch can offer significant savings. Substitution of one or two electrically powered fans can also offer substantial savings.

Not much can be done to reduce the power used by the alternator or power steering, but we can use a switch to shut the air conditioner off during acceleration or when climbing hills and mountains. The overall savings may not be great. The additional power available for climbing and acceleration can be significant if power is minimal during this condition.

PARASITIC POWER LOSSES

Parasitic engine power losses are frequently overlooked. We read a lot about losses due to back pressure in the exhaust system, but little about losses due to intake restrictions. Most engines used in RVs can benefit from a dual exhaust system and free-flowing mufflers. <u>RX for RV Performance and Mileage</u> by John Geraghty and Bill Estes has a good discussion of this topic with recommendations for most popular RV engines.

Mostly overlooked, however, are power losses due to intake restrictions. It is commonly thought that one air filter is as good as another. Not so. In a test, it was found that the best filters had about half the air restriction of the second best which, in turn, had half the restriction of the third best. Surprisingly, the least restrictive filter was also best at removing contaminants from the air. Check to see how much air your filter will flow. You might be surprised. Engine power is directly related to quantity of air consumed. Any restriction decreases power.

Since axle and transmission losses account for 72% of powertrain losses, they also offer large potential savings. Use of synthetic lubricants can be important in both transmissions and differentials as well as wheel bearings. Synthetics cost more than their petroleum counterparts, but they last longer and are more free-flowing. The difference is even greater in cold weather. There is some evidence of increased mileage from using synthetic engine oil, too.

An area that offers lots of potential for fuel savings but also generates lots of controversy is engine size/differential gear ratio selection. We would all like to have a combination of engine size and gear ratio that would permit us to climb the steepest grade at 55 to 60 and still deliver 20 mpg. We all know that isn't possible. We also know that some combinations we might want are not available due to governmental restrictions. But we can still make choices that will improve performance and efficiency.

ENGINE EFFICIENCIES

We need to start with an understanding of engine efficiency. Engines tend to give their highest fuel efficiency when operating near their peak torque rpm. For most of the engines we use, that is in the range of 2200 to 2600 rpm. Theoretically, we should gear so that at cruising speed the engine is turning at peak torque speed. Unfortunately, some of the engines we try to use don't develop enough horsepower to pull our RVs at that speed. So we choose a differential ratio with a higher number and let the engine turn at a higher rpm. The result is more noise, greater engine wear and more fuel burned.

Truckers take a different approach. They insist on an engine that will handle the load at the speed they want to travel under normal, level road conditions. Then they select a gear ratio that will let the engine turn at peak torque rpm at that road speed. When the grade or wind don't permit travel at that engine speed in top gear, they drop down a gear. In most cases, we can't drop down a gear quite so easily. For one thing, we are usually limited to three or four speeds in our transmissions. The trucker may have 13 or more speeds. He can drop down a gear and only increase engine speed 100 rpm while maintaining the same road speed. Or he can maintain his rpm and accept the slight decrease in road speed.

We can get nearly the same benefits by using overdrives or underdrives. Either one will double the number of speeds available and give greater driving flexibility. Let's look at a couple of examples.

First, consider the problem of towing a trailer. The tow vehicle is likely used most of the time as just transportation without the trailer. Okay, select an engine with the power needed to pull the trailer at good road speed at its peak torque rpm. Then select a differential ratio that provides that road speed at that rpm while the transmission is in top gear. That provides the cruising performance desired while towing. Add an overdrive for improved mileage when the trailer is not hooked up. With an automatic, you then have a six-speed transmission with five of those speeds available for towing.

With a four-speed transmission, you have an eight-speed combination with seven speeds for towing. Both offer the option of dropping down from top gear to second or third and overdrive for additional power when needed for climbing or bucking a wind. And both offer all the other combinations for greater efficiency while climbing. There is no rule that says that you have to run in the top gear on your transmission. The rule that the truckers have found works best is to gear fast and run slow. That is, select a combination of engine and gearing that permits the desired road speed at a peak torque engine speed. Save those high engine rpm for accelerating and climbing.

MOTORHOME UNDERDRIVE

A motorhome has a different situation. Here the operation is always under load. It would make sense to gear a motorhome to run in the top gear at the desired road speed with the engine turning at peak torque rpm. Add an underdrive for increased pulling power when climbing or bucking a wind. With an underdrive, you have either six or eight speeds, all useful for driving depending upon the road conditions. Again, there is no reason not to run in third gear and underdrive if the conditions warrant.

Most of us RVers come from a background of driving cars or light trucks under situations that seldom require down-shifting. We expect to climb all hills in top gear and would never dream of driving down the road at a lower gear. Truckers run in the gear that is appropriate for the load and road conditions. We need to remember that while driving our RVs, we are driving heavy equipment, too, and we should adopt driving practices that fit.

It may surprise you to learn that the one factor in the Peterbilt study that had the greatest potential for fuel savings was the driver. Using high engine speeds wastes fuel whether it is done through improper gearing, needlessly fast acceleration, driving too fast, or shifting at engine speeds higher than necessary. The result is the same -- wasted fuel. The driver wastes fuel, too, by not anticipating stops. Trucks and RVs are heavy vehicles. They take time to stop. Beginning stops earlier than you would in an unloaded car saves fuel and extends brake life.

PETERBILT'S STUDY

In summary, the recommendations from the Peterbilt study were:

1. Drive at a reasonable speed. Each mph over 55 increases fuel requirements by 1.5 to 2.5%. Even the best drivers will find their speed varying by a few mph. A cruise control will help improve mileage.

2. Gear fast and run slow. Select and use gearing that permits your engine to run at its most efficient speed. Use a vacuum gauge to help you stay just above the enrichment point of your carburetor.

3. Improve your aerodynamics by using properly designed and placed deflectors and other devices to improve airflow. Select an RV with rounded corners, and stay away from rear bunkhouse arrangements. Select an RV with an upward slope to the roof at the front. Install roof pods only when necessary and minimize their frontal area.

4. Use radial tires if you can and keep them inflated to the highest pressure recommended by the manufacturer. Check inflation pressures frequently.

5. Follow a good maintenance program. A properly maintained vehicle burns less fuel. Use synthetic lubricants in the transmission and differential when possible. Select low-restriction air filters.

What can you expect to get from following these recommendations? Obviously, conditions vary. Some vehicles are inherently more efficient than others. But Peterbilt found that you can expect to get from 10% to 31% improvement. The divisions among rolling resistance, aerodynamics and powertrain potentials were about even, with aerodynamics offering slightly more than the others.

With my own RV, I was able to realize 10% improvement in mpg with powertrain improvements. I haven't started my program to improve aerodynamics. I fully expect another 10% there.

That hasn't doubled my mileage, I know. But if all of us try different methods and pass the results along, we can make significant improvements. If we will insist that RV manufacturers use information from studies such as the one by Peterbilt, we can expect greater efficiency designed into the RVs we buy. Put it all together, and we should reasonably expect at least a 50% improvement. The truckers are getting it. Why shouldn't we?

Chapter 29

A Turbocharger Makes Your Diesel Move

There's an old saying that when you want power, there is no substitute for inches. Meaning that if you want more power, you have to have a larger engine. Well, things have changed. Now there is a substitute for inches.

Sometimes we forget just why a larger engine develops more power and torque than a smaller engine. Some engineers would have us believe that the laws of thermodynamics have been repealed. Let's take a brief look at how an engine makes power.

Every time we stop at the fuel pump, we are reminded that power means fuel burned. But fuel won't burn without oxygen. Oxygen comes from the air, so let's just say that an engine needs air and fuel to make power. How the engine gets its air is important in determining the amount of power it can develop. Each time a piston moves down on an intake stroke, we say it draws in a cylinder full of air. Not much of that statement is really true.

What happens is this: Air surrounds us and the engine constantly. It may not feel like it, but air has weight. We talk about the weight of air as air pressure. At sea level, air pressure is about 14 pounds per square inch. As we climb above sea level the pressure decreases.

CYLINDER NOT FULL

Now back to the engine. When the piston moves down on an intake stroke, the pressure of the atmospheric air -- the air that surrounds us -- pushes air into the cylinder. If the piston moves very slowly, the cylinder may be completely filled. But when an engine is running at cruising speed, the piston is moving so fast that the air pressure is not great enough to fill the cylinder completely.

In actual practice, a naturally aspirated engine -- one that depends on atmospheric pressure to fill the cylinders -- gets only about an 80% fill. Engineers say it has a volumetric efficiency of 80%. What matters to us is that our 8-liter wonder engine doesn't burn 8 liters of air; it burns 80% of 8 liters or 6.4 liters. That makes a lot of difference, since the amount of power an engine develops is directly proportional to the amount of air it burns.

The problem gets worse in the mountains. The engine still burns 6.4 liters of air, but the air is so much thinner that the results are the same as if the engine were burning only, say, 5 liters of air.

It would be nice if there was some way to make sure that 8-liter engine burned a full 8 liters of air whenever we wanted it to whether at sea level or driving over Wolf Creek Pass. Fortunately, there is a way to do that and more.

ENTER THE SUPERCHARGER

Superchargers, in one form or another, have been around longer than internal combustion engines. A supercharger is nothing more than a pump. One early application in the middle 1800s was to force additional air into blast furnaces to increase the heat and burning efficiency of the furnaces. The supercharger does the same thing for internal combustion engines.

(Don't worry that I've switched to talking about superchargers. There's a reason, and I'll get back to turbochargers in a few minutes.)

Early engineers were aware of the limitations of naturally aspirated engines and experimented with various kinds of high volume air pumps to force additional air into the engines. The results were both effective and troublesome. As long as the pumps worked, the engines did develop greater power. But designing a reliable system for driving the pumps was difficult. It took nearly 40 years to find the answer. By that time, other engineers had further improved the engines themselves to the degree that superchargers were no longer as important.

Then came the realization that our gasoline and diesel engines were high on the list of polluters of the air we breathe. By governmental fiat, engines were forced to be more efficient. Engines shrank in size, and compression ratios plummeted. Those of us who needed gobs of power were in real trouble. Then someone remembered superchargers.

TYPES OF SUPERCHARGERS

There are several types of superchargers. The two main ones are the Roots-type blowers used for decades on big diesel trucks and centrifugal blowers. Centrifugal superchargers had been used briefly back in the Thirties, but the gear drives necessary to achieve the very high blower speeds had proved troublesome.

World War II had shown another way of driving centrifugal blowers on aircraft engines. Some of the burnt exhaust gases were routed through a turbine. The expanding gases spun the turbine at high speed. A centrifugal blower was attached to the turbine shaft and the turbocharger was born. (See, I told you I'd get back.) The result was a supercharger that ran on almost free power.

Turbochargers have been mated to so many different engines in the past 10 years that they have lost their exotic flavor. But one of the most interesting applications of turbochargers has been on diesel engines. Diesels have long been noted for their fuel efficiency and long life. All large trucks are powered by diesels. In the race to improve fuel efficiency that began in the Seventies, diesel popularity briefly soared.

The popularity was brief because users discovered another diesel trait. The beasts may have power, but they are slow. Generations of drivers accustomed to the quick acceleration of high-powered gasoline engines weren't about to accept the more leisurely response of diesels. And, of course, there was GM's ill-fated venture with its Oldsmobile gasoline-to-diesel conversion.

GOOD DIESELS DEVELOPED

Fortunately for us RVers, both GM and Ford decided to try a little harder. Both developed small truck-size diesels with real diesel design. (Okay, so Ford went to International to get its engine.) The popularity of the two engines was both immediate and gratifying. But the problem of slow throttle response was still a handicap in many owners' minds. They also wanted more power.

Turbocharger engineers and manufacturers quickly joined the fray. The result was a marriage made in heaven. Well, maybe Dearborn. Diesels and turbochargers were made for each other. With the turbocharger capable of boosting intake pressure by several pounds, the volumetric efficiency of the engines jumped.

Now it was theoretically possible to turn the 8-liter engine into a 12-liter engine when needed. How? Well remember back to the beginning. The atmospheric pressure at sea level is 14 pounds. Add to that 7 pounds of boost from the turbo, and theoretically the engine can be stuffed with 12 liters of air. It's like increasing the size of the engine by 50%.

Well, we all know how theory often departs from reality, but in this case the difference is not so great. In actual practice, it is not unusual for addition of a turbocharger to give 40% to 50% greater power to the diesel engine. That's a lot of help. There's more.

FUEL EFFICIENCY INCREASES

Because the turbocharger also assures that all cylinders are equally charged with air, fuel efficiency increases slightly under load. No-load condition mileage remains about the same. There is also the possibility of significantly increasing load fuel economy by using the engine's most efficient speed. Diesel engines are designed to run slower than gasoline engines. Best fuel economy is attained at or near peak torque speed.

With the Ford 7.3-liter engine, for example, best fuel economy can be expected at an engine speed of about 2,200 rpm. The problem is that with a normally aspirated engine there isn't enough power at that speed to give the desired performance. Using a turbocharger increases the power available at lower speeds sufficiently that it is often practical to gear for a cruising engine speed of 2,200 to 2,300 rpm rather than the 2,600 rpm needed without the turbo. Fuel economy will show an increase due to the more efficient engine speed.

Turbocharger impellers run at very high speeds. Proper lubrication is important. So is turbocharger temperature. Some turbo installations on gasoline engines have suffered from "cokeing" when the engine is turned off without letting the turbo cool down. The turbo is extremely hot and literally cooks the lubricating oil in the bearings into a hard substance similar to coke. Early bearing failure is the result.

According to Jerry Lagod, president of Hypermax Engineering, that is not a problem with turbos on diesels. "Gasoline exhaust temperatures are much higher than diesels. Diesel exhaust temperatures also decrease very rapidly when the engine idles. It is only necessary to idle the engine for about a minute after a hard climb to cool the turbo down. When stopping at a roadside on a level run, there is no need to cool down."

DIESELS RUN COOLER

Steve Benson, designer of the Advanced Turbo Systems turbocharger, credits the turbo with making diesel engines run cooler as well as more efficiently. Diesels always operate with excess air passing through the cylinders. The amount of power generated is determined by the amount of fuel injected. Using a turbo increases the amount of air available and permits a higher setting of the fuel injector pump and still retain an air surplus.

According to Gale Banks Engineering, this excess of air typically lowers the exhaust gas temperature under cruise conditions from 600 to 650 degrees for normally aspirated engines to 400 degrees for turbocharged engines. Lower exhaust gas temperatures also mean that pistons and valves are running cooler and that engine life can be expected to increase.

Turbochargers are available as both engineered kits for specific engines and as do-it-yourself installations using parts available from suppliers. The safer approach is to use a kit designed for your specific engine. The engineering has been done for you, the parts are made for the specific application, and you know the kit is going to fit.

A turbocharger kit can be purchased from any of the three main builders of kits or from their dealers. A skillful mechanic could probably install one of the kits himself in 10 to 12 hours. Or the dealers can make the complete installation for you. Which to do depends on your skills and the facilities you have available. I can only suggest that you assess your situation carefully. Installing a turbocharger kit is more complicated than changing the engine oil or installing a new water pump.

NOW FACTORY-DIRECT

Many prospective diesel owners have wondered why they couldn't buy a turbocharged engine directly from the factory. Now you can. Beginning with the 1989 model year, Dodge offered the 5.9-liter Cummins turbocharged diesel as an option on selected models of their pickups. And also beginning with 1989 models, the Banks turbocharger is available on certain models of the GMC 6.2 diesel through GMC dealers. Once the truck is built, it is delivered to the Banks installation center nearby. Banks installs the turbocharger, checks it out, and returns the truck to the GMC plant for delivery to the customer.

A turbocharger on your GM or Ford diesel can significantly increase your truck's towing ability. One indication of the effect of turbocharging can be found in the fact that nearly all over-the-road diesel trucks are turbocharged.

Chapter 30

Upper Cylinder Lubricants: New Look At An Old Idea

It's a rough world inside the combustion chambers of your engine. Temperatures run to hundreds of degrees. Pressures rise and everything happens at blinding speeds. And think of the friction. Pistons move up and down in the cylinders at up to 2,600 feet per minute, and there's never time to cool down until the engine stops. Then it just sits there cooking in all that heat. It's a rough world. And we expect the engine to go on and on for a hundred thousand miles or more with limited attention. When you stop to think about it, it's a wonder the poor engine doesn't just cough and say, "That's all, folks. I quit."

To make the problem worse, there is limited lubrication in that cruel world. There is plenty of lubrication to engine bearings. Oil pressure sees to that. But the only oil that gets to the upper cylinder area gets there by accident.

Engineers try their best to keep oil out of the upper cylinder. Oil control rings are designed expressly to keep oil from getting into the combustion chamber. A small amount of oil is sprayed on cylinder walls below the piston as the piston moves up on the compression and exhaust strokes, but that oil is immediately scraped off as the piston moves back down. A very small amount also gets into the combustion area by sneaking past the valve guides, but careful fitting of seals tries to prevent that as much as possible. When the engine is turned off, most of the residual oil on the valve stems and cylinder walls drains down. The result is that on start-up, valve stems and guides, pistons and cylinders operate in a basically unlubricated condition. This condition lasts until the oil is warmed up enough to spray and leak past the seals. Engine wear during the few minutes of warmup on a cold morning may be greater than many thousands of miles of travel at high speeds after warmup.

PISTON-WALL OIL DIRTY

Another difficulty in the equation is that the oil that does manage to make it to piston walls and the combustion chamber is dirty. Because piston rings that are insufficiently lubricated do not seal completely, products of combustion are blown past the rings and added to the oil that circulates throughout the engine. Those combustion products are mainly carbon and water, but there are others such as sulphur and unburned additives in the fuel. These combine in the crankcase to form sludge and sulfuric acid. The sludge can plug oil passages. Sulfuric acid slowly dissolves metal. Neither situation is good.

Another effect of the dirty oil that is often overlooked is hard and soft carbon that forms in the combustion chamber. Burned fuel is usually blamed for carbon formation, but fuel may not be the real culprit. More likely, the carbon is formed when contaminated oil that sneaks past the piston rings is superheated in the combustion chambers. Heat causes the carbon in the contaminated oil to become sticky and adhere to combustion chamber walls. Continued heat from burning fuel hardens the deposits. The deposits retain heat after fuel has burned and form hot spots that can, in turn, induce precombustion of the next bit of incoming fuel. Precombustion is one big reason for loss of engine power, pinging, and severe engine damage.

As I said, it's a tough world in an engine's upper cylinder area, but it gets even tougher. Until recently, lead compounds in gasoline furnished essential lubrication to the sealing area between valve faces and valve seats. The lead, added to gasoline to improve anti-knock characteristics, was deposited in minuscule amounts to the valve faces and seats. This kept the valves and valve seats from making iron-to-iron contact. That becomes very important when engines are operating under heavy-duty conditions.

BUT LEAD IS DISAPPEARING

Now that lead has been removed from gasoline, the valves and seats are no longer separated by lead deposits. During the time that valves are closed on the compression stroke, the metal-to-metal contact can reach such high temperatures that tiny welds form between valves and valve seats. When the valves are forced open, the welds are broken and tiny pieces are torn from either the valve face or valve seats. In a short time, the torn areas permit burning gases from combustion to leak past and burn out larger areas. Engineers call this valve recession. The rest of us call it valve burning. Either way, you can call it expensive.

Studies by the Environmental Protection Agency have shown that valve recession with unleaded fuel can severely damage engines in a very short time when those engines are operating under heavy-duty conditions. Those are conditions reached by such as trucks, farm tractors and RV engines. The situation is serious enough that the EPA is trying to find some way of providing farmers with leaded gasoline. No one but RVers is interested in the problems of RVers.

Why not just use leaded fuel in our RVs? Well, for one thing, it's illegal for most of us. Our RVs were built with catalytic converters to clean up the air, and it's illegal to remove the converters. For another, finding leaded fuel is becoming more and more difficult. Soon it will be impossible.

Now for the good news. There are a few white knights still riding around out there. A couple of them have been around for some 70 years and are well-proven. I've been using one of them for several years and recently had the opportunity to test another.

UPPER CYLINDER LUBRICANTS

The use of upper cylinder lubricants is an old idea. Lubrication engineers figured out a long time ago that the easiest way to lubricate the combustion chamber, valve stems and faces, and the upper cylinder area was to supply the lubricant with the fuel. That way it is fed automatically to the very area that needs the lubrication. Because the lubricant is mixed with the fuel, the lubricant is supplied immediately on start-up. As soon as fuel is drawn into the cylinder, lubricant coats the cylinder walls and valves.

The best upper cylinder lubricants use high flash oil bases. Because they resist burning, they are deposited on all of the surfaces, including the piston head and piston rings. One result is better sealing of the piston rings. This, in turn, results in less leakage past the rings, better compression, less blow-by of contaminants and less friction. Also, because of the better ring seal, there are fewer deposits from contaminated engine oil in the combustion chambers and less carbon buildup.

Those are most of the claims that have been made for upper cylinder lubricants for 70 years. Until the removal of lead from gasoline, those were enough. Now there is interest in the lubrication of valve faces and seats. From the experience of fleet users, it appears that the best of these products furnish sufficient lubrication to the valve sealing areas to largely eliminate the problem of valve recession due to lack of lead.

As I mentioned, I've been using one of the products for years. There are two ways of getting upper cylinder lubrication into the engine. The one I've been using contains a metering system that feeds a tiny amount of lubricant from a reservoir into the intake manifold. From there, it is carried by the incoming fuel mixture to the upper cylinders.

I have liked the convenience, but I have always been a little concerned that the lubricant might not be equally distributed to all cylinders. The problem, if there is one, is that entry of the lubricant into the intake manifold is at a position dependent on a vacuum attachment point that may not be near the center of the manifold. If the attachment point is offset significantly, it seems that some cylinders might not be getting sufficient product to assure the lubrication I'm after.

ADDED TO THE GASOLINE

The second method eliminates that problem by mixing the lubricant with gasoline in the fuel tank. A small quantity is simply added to the fuel tank along with gasoline. It mixes with the gasoline and is held in suspension. All cylinders receive their share of lubricant. The trade-off is one of better distribution of lubricant at some slight inconvenience. It is one of these products, LubriGas, that I recently tested.

I have long been sold on the need for an upper cylinder lubricant. I believed that the most important result of using such a product was the improved lubrication and decreased engine wear. I still believe that. It never occurred to me that there might be fuel mileage improvements.

When I was approached by the LubriGas representative with a request to test his product, I was reluctant. How do you show any results if the results are only longer engine life? I couldn't tear down the engine, measure wear surfaces, drive the engine for 100,000 miles, tear it down and remeasure. To show any kind of results would require doing the process on two identical engines, one with and one without the product, used in identical service. Impossible for me.

But the LubriGas people also claim that improved lubrication results in less friction which results in better fuel mileage. I could test that. So, on a cold day in November I did a mileage test using an engine that had not been treated with any upper cylinder lubricant.

ROAD TEST PROVES OUT

I topped off the tank and drove a 70-mile circuit on the expressway. To maintain consistency, I used cruise control and drove the speed limit when traffic would allow. About two-thirds of the distance was at 55 mph with the rest at 65. I used 4.6 gallons for an average of 15.2 miles per gallon. After carefully topping the tank and adding four ounces of LubriGas, I drove the circuit again. To be honest, I figured I was just exercising my truck. When I completed the circuit and topped the tank it would take only 4.4 gallons for an average of 15.9 mpg. That's an improvement of 4.6%. I believe that's a significant improvement. But I also believe that all of the benefits of upper cylinder lubrication are cumulative. The fuel mileage difference should get better for a while as I continue to use LubriGas.

LubriGas is mainly sold to fleet users -- those companies that run hundreds of cars, trucks and buses. One of their customers has over 1,000 vehicles in its fleet. Those customers buy LubriGas by the 55-gallon drum. That would be an absurd quantity for most of us. Fortunately, LubriGas also sells the product in smaller quantities. They have a package of one gallon and one quart for $26. The quart is a graduated container with a convenient pour spout. That quantity of LubriGas is enough to treat 625 gallons of gasoline. The cost figures to 4 cents per gallon of gasoline.

One large fleet user's records show a mileage improvement of 10%. If you average 10 mpg and gasoline costs $1 a gallon, your fuel cost is 10 cents per mile. If you get a 10% improvement with LubriGas, your fuel cost at $1.04 a gallon is down to 9.5 cents per mile. The LubriGas has paid for itself. The extra engine life is free. It's fun to test a product that does exactly what it claims to do.

Does that smell like a bargain? Contact LubriGas at L/G Formulators, P.O. Box 429, Fraser, Detroit, Michigan 48026.

Chapter 31

Used RVs Can Save You Money

There's nothing wrong with buying a brand new RV if you can afford it, but there are lots of reasons why a used one might be better for you. Obviously, a used motorhome or trailer will cost less than a new one of the same model. But cost is only one factor to consider.

Many first-time RV buyers have only a vague idea of what it's like to own and use an RV. They tend to compare an RV with the cottage they rented last year. They look at the 800 square feet of the cottage and decide that an RV would have to be that large. Then they discover that even a 35-foot trailer has less than 280 square feet. The decision, then, is to buy the biggest RV they can find.

Conversely, they might decide, arbitrarily, that they can get by with a very small RV because they don't intend to use it often or because they can obviously purchase a small unit for a lot less cash.

The next step is predictable. Our new RVers discover that RV living is totally different from cottage living and their new, expensive toy is either much too large or much too small for their needs. Or they find out that a different floorplan would be more comfortable. Or any one of a dozen things that should be different. A slightly used RV is for sale.

LEARN RVING WITH USED RIG

The same lessons could have been learned for a lot less money by buying a used RV. Most people will be better served if their first RV were a used one. Less money has been spent in learning what RVing is about. If a mistake in original choice was made, the lesson is not so expensive.

Not all used RVs are bought by first-time purchasers. Many RVers have learned that they can buy a luxury model used RV for less than a new one of lower quality. Some of these buyers will own several RVs over the years without ever seeing the need to plunk down money for a new one. I've owned eight trailers since 1955. Only three were purchased new. Buying used gave me the chance to try different sizes without spending a fortune. To tell the truth, if some hadn't been bought used, I wouldn't have been able to afford an RV.

To find out what is presently available in used RVs, I visited with Bruce Wilson of Advance Camping Sales in Milwaukee. Advance has been selling RVs for many years and has a large stock of used trailers and motorhomes as well as a quality repair facility. Some dealers don't like to handle used equipment, but Bruce said, "Used RVs are great for us. We sell 50 to 80 a year."

The models we looked at are probably typical of what can be found at any large RV dealer. In looking around the lot, I found seven units that were representative of the variety. The newest we looked at -- there obviously were newer ones on the lot -- was a 25-foot 1986 Franklin trailer with front kitchen and dinette, center living room, permanent rear bed and bath and air conditioning. It was a clean trailer that no one would apologize for owning at $7,900.

ALL SIZES, PRICES

The shopper looking for a larger trailer could have spotted a 32-foot 1981 Yellowstone that looked as clean as new. It had air conditioning, sub-floor ducted heat, convenient bunkhouse sleeping for the kids and an awning. Asking price, $9,500.

At the opposite end of the size and price range was a clean and neat 17-foot 1975 Fleetwing with front dinette. The trailer could be towed by nearly any six-cylinder tow vehicle. At an asking price of $2,995 some family could have several wonderful, fun-filled years of RVing.

Motorhomes are also available. I looked at two Class C's. One was a 26-foot 1984 Mallard with air conditioning and generator. Clean and in excellent condition with good tires, Bruce was asking $22,499.

The second Class C was a 26-foot 1984 Yellowstone with a Ford 460 engine, less than 20,000 miles and air conditioning. It could hardly be told from new. It could be yours for $25,900.

RELIABILITY OF DEALER

What else do you get with a used RV? All units sold by reliable dealers get a full safety check. If tires are questionable, they are replaced. Propane and water systems are checked for leaks. All appliances are checked for safety and proper operation.

Appliance operation is important. Anyone can learn in a couple of minutes whether the range and water pump work. But it takes at least 24 hours to see whether the refrigerator cools down the way it should. Checking the refrigerator burner for operation is not enough. Many RVers abuse their refrigerators by not parking on the level. Most propane-powered refrigerators can be ruined in about a day of unlevel operation. The burner will still work, but the unit will not get cold. The cost of replacing a refrigerator can run to over $1,500, depending on size. That's enough to ruin your vacation.

The possibility of major appliance repair is a factor in considering where you buy your used RV and the kind of warranty you get. Reputable dealers will either offer a warranty or tell you what's wrong with the RV and reflect the deficiencies in the price. Most warranties will be for 90 days.

Checking the ads in the Sunday paper will quickly show you that dealers are not the only ones who sell used RVs. Every spring and summer, there are hundreds of privately owned RVs listed for sale. Most of them will sell for less than if sold by a dealer. You can save important bucks buying that way. Or you can lose a bundle.

CHECK UNIT CAREFULLY

No private owner is in a position to offer a warranty. Unless you know the seller, you have no way of knowing the real condition of the RV. Sure, you see if it has been scratched or crashed. But you can't know the condition of the refrigerator or how many miles it has been driven down Rough Canyon Road. That's not to say that you should never buy a used RV from anyone but a dealer. I've bought two trailers from private owners. I was both careful and lucky.

To help improve your luck in buying a used RV from either a dealer or private owner, here are some suggestions. First, I would never consider buying from a dealer who did not have a repair facility. It's too easy to get into -- and out of -- the used RV business if all you need is an empty lot and a portable office. Such a dealer will expect to get the usual dealer's markup but can offer little in the way of a warranty.

Approach a used RV the same way you would a house and car. The RV has many of the same systems and potential problems of both. Overall outside condition will tell a lot about the way the unit has been treated. Unrepaired tears in the surfaces suggest a careless owner. Look at the tires the same way you would with a car. Tires are expensive. If they need to be replaced, factor that into the price. Look underneath the unit. There should be no dangling wires or pipes and no indication of damage to axles, springs, or frame. Out front, the propane bottles and rack should be free from serious rust. The jack post and hitch socket should show no signs of damage.

LOOK INSIDE FOR ABUSE

Inside, look for general condition to be free from abuse. An RV is lived in and can be expected to show signs of having been used. But deep gouges in the paneling, torn upholstery, missing cabinet hardware and other signs of abuse serve as caution signals. I've seen RVs five or more years old that look hardly used. Others appear to have been through a war zone. I know which one I don't want at any price.

Test as many systems as possible. Lights should work. If the weather is warm, insist on putting water in the tank and checking the plumbing for operation and leaks. Look in the bottom cabinets where water lines lead for signs of leaks. Check the refrigerator and sink for cleanliness just as you would in a house.

Mattresses are expensive to replace. Check for serious stains and tears in the fabric. Check to see that mattress pads are in the folding overhead bunks, if any. Some people take the pads out and use the bunks for storage.

Checking the propane system and refrigerator are the trickiest parts of the inspection. Often there will be no gas in the bottles. If you're buying from a private owner, ask to have the gas turned on. If there is any reluctance and you like the RV enough to be seriously interested, offer to fill a bottle. Then check for leaks at ALL gas line joints with liquid soap and a small brush. A small leak is no cause for rejecting the unit if the leaky joint can be easily repaired. Most can be.

OPERATE APPLIANCES

Light the range burners and see that they maintain a good, blue flame. Don't light the water heater unless it has been filled with water. Light the refrigerator and arrange to check it for proper cooling after 24 hours. The fact that the burner appears to be working properly is no indication that the unit will cool.

Light the furnace. Within a few minutes it should be warming the interior. Inspect all panels for signs of water leaks. Look especially carefully around roof vents and windows. Any stains in these areas are strong signals of possible trouble.

An owner probably won't let you tow test a trailer, but any motorhome should certainly be driven. Check the same things you would on a car. While a motorhome will not be as agile as your Corvette, it should move out with enough indication of power that you would feel comfortable on steep hills. Brakes and transmission should operate properly. All electrical systems should work. Don't forget to check the air conditioner even if the weather is cold. Steering should be tight with no indication of pulling to one side. After driving a few miles, inspect under the hood and under the unit for leaks in fuel, oil, cooling and brake systems. All of these can be repaired, but some repairs can be costly. If you have questions, check with your friendly mechanic about possible problems and repair costs.

Finally, if you like the RV and it looks as if it fits your needs, begin the bargaining over price. The price of every RV is negotiable. Comparing the asking price with the "book price" is not as easy with an RV as with a truck or car, but a dealer or your banker should be able to give you an indication of average prices for the model and year. But don't be afraid to pay a little extra for an especially nice unit that fits your needs.

Buying a used RV can be an interesting and profitable experience. I think everyone's first RV should have seen service before. Owning one is the least expensive way to find out what the RV life is like and what kind of RV is best suited to you.

Chapter 32

Vapor Lock And How to Deal With It

Unless you drive a diesel, the odds are excellent that you have either experienced vapor lock or that you will. More than one-fourth of the energy in every gallon of gasoline your engine burns is converted directly to heat. Another third goes out the exhaust system. A lot of that is also heat. In the winter, engine-generated heat is a blessing. In the summer, it can be a curse.

Engineers try to arrange things so that heat passes out of the engine compartment, under the vehicle and out into the air. The process works only fairly well in pickups. In vans and motorhomes, it doesn't work nearly so well. The heat tends to get trapped in the engine compartment. Some of it finds its way through the walls of the compartment and into the passenger area. We turn on the air conditioner, which adds more heat to the engine compartment. Some of that heat surrounds the fuel lines and causes problems as either heat soak or vapor lock. The effects and cures are similar.

Gasoline begins to vaporize at about 86 degrees F. The temperature around an engine is usually much higher. Fortunately, when gasoline is pressurized, the vaporizing temperature rises. When the engine is running, the fuel pump normally keeps the fuel between the pump and the carburetor sufficiently pressurized to prevent it from vaporizing.

But if you've been driving for a while and stop for a break, everything in the engine compartment gets deep soaked with engine heat. Gasoline in the carburetor is not under pressure, and it quickly reaches vaporization temperature. Some of the fuel boils off. In some instances, the carburetor boils dry. When you come back and try to start the engine, the carburetor has no fuel and the engine won't start.

VAPORIZED FUEL LINE GAS

Some of the heat also vaporizes the gasoline in the fuel line and in the fuel pump. Mechanical fuel pumps, the kind installed in most vehicles, are not good at pumping vapor. No matter how much you run the starter, the pump can't pump fuel to the carburetor. After several tries, the battery is dead and your temperature has reached the boiling point so you are experiencing your own vapor lock.

As many of you have discovered, you don't have to be parked to experience vapor lock. Engine heat soaks into the fuel pump. The pump may get so hot that the gasoline turns to vapor and the pump can't work. Some of the heat soaks into the fuel line between the tank and the pump, vaporizing the fuel. More bad news.

What can you do? Heat is the problem. A temporary solution that may get you started is to pour cold water on the fuel pump. If it is going to work at all, a quart will be enough. Some owners have even installed a water tank, windshield washer pump and a switch just to cool the pump. Others have had success fabricating an air deflector to direct more cooling air onto the pump.

While the water treatment may get you started, it is only treating the symptom. It's like taking an aspirin to relieve a headache caused by eyestrain. The eyes still strain and the headache will return.

REDUCE HEAT NEAR FUEL SYSTEM

Heat around the fuel system must be reduced. Start by installing a 180-degree thermostat. That will also help alleviate an engine's tendency to ping. Check your fan clutch to make sure it is doing its job. Some people insulate the fuel line from the pump to the carburetor. Cagle Corporation, 2667 E. 28th St. Suite 517, Long Beach, CA 90806, makes an insulating tape that is not bulky and is easy to apply.

Relocating fuel lines to keep them as far as possible from exhaust pipes and manifolds is always a good idea. The classic solution has been to install an electric fuel pump and filter as near the fuel tank as possible. Get one with a large capacity at normal fuel pressures. I used a Holley #65-12801. It's noisy but it works. You can get one either new or rebuilt at any parts store. Electric power to the pump must be routed through an oil pressure switch so that the pump will only work when the engine is running.

An additional treatment that is almost certain to give relief is to install a vapor return line from the carburetor to the fuel tank. The idea is to furnish a way to remove the vapor and to keep some fuel continually circulating through the system. That way the fuel in the lines can't get so hot. Look at it this way: If you get 10 miles per gallon and are driving 60 miles per hour, it takes ten minutes for a gallon of fuel to pass through the lines. That's slow. During that time, the fuel soaks up a lot of heat. By continually circulating the fuel, it doesn't have time to get so hot.

Ford makes a vapor separator valve that can be installed in the fuel line at the carburetor. Ask for part #E3TZ9N176-B. Use a fuel-approved neoprene line from the separator down to the vehicle frame and copper or aluminum from there back to the tank. Be sure the lines are kept away from engine and exhaust heat sources and are securely attached so that they can not be damaged.

With all of that, you should have no more trouble with vapor lock.

Chapter 33

Weight, GVWR, Payload and Safety

A lot of RVers seem to get very confused and complacent about the Gross Vehicle Weight Ratings (GVWR) of their rigs. They might be in for a painful and expensive surprise. As an example, I recently found one expensive Class A motorhome that had no weight capacity left for such things as food, clothing, personal items and passengers by the time the tanks were filled. Interesting, no?

The designed GVWR is the maximum weight that engineers have decided the chassis can safely carry. In computing the GVWR, engineers look at such things as the strength of the frame, capacity of the springs, weight-carrying ability of the axles, strength and design of the wheels and the size of the tires. Ideally, all elements will have about the same ratings.

The engineers also have to consider such things as weight distribution over the chassis. In most motorhomes, the bulk of the weight is centered in the rear half or two-thirds of the coach. The engineers make an estimate of the distribution and select front and rear axles to match their estimates.

For example, one popular Class C chassis with a GVWR of 11,500 pounds has a front axle rating of 4,200 pounds and a rear axle rating of 8,000 pounds. If you add those two figures, they give a total axle rating of 12,200 pounds versus a total chassis rating of 11,500 pounds. Where did the other 700 pounds go? Checking further, we find that the front and rear springs have a total rating of 12,000 pounds. That still leaves 500 pounds unaccounted for.

Some motorhome manufacturers using this same chassis list the GVWR of their coaches as high as 12,800 pounds. Ask them about the discrepancy, and they will tell you they have "rerated" the chassis. It would seem that the motorhome builder believes he knows more about the strength of the chassis than does the chassis manufacturer.

Also, some coach builders lengthen the chassis, put a second rear (tag) axle under it, and rate the chassis at 15,000 pounds.

With the same idea in mind, some owners install tires with greater weight-carrying capacity and helper springs or air bags and think they have increased the GVWR of their motorhome. They have the same axles, wheels and frame they started with. Something's gotta give, and in many instances it does sooner or later.

Another important weight figure is the unloaded or dry weight of the RV. The difference between that weight and the GVWR is referred to as the payload. The payload is the maximum amount of weight you can add without exceeding the designed, safe carrying capacity of the unit. It includes such things as water and oil in the engine, engine fuel, propane, water, food, clothing, personal items. And, oh yes, passengers. Approximate figures you can use for computing payload are 8 pounds per gallon of water, 6 pounds per gallon of gasoline, and 7 pounds per gallon of propane. These aren't exact, but they are close enough. Don't forget to include the weight of the propane tank(s). Figure 30 pounds for each tank as a starting point. Have you got a generator? Figure that weight, too.

Let's look at some actual numbers. One Class C coach by a large manufacturer lists a GVWR of 11,000 pounds and a dry weight of 9,900 pounds. It has a 30-gallon fresh water tank, carries 19 gallons of propane, and a 6-gallon water heater. That amounts to 444 pounds. Fill the gas tanks for another 240 pounds. That leaves 416 pounds for your family, food, clothing and personal items. If you also have the optional generator, knock off another 200 pounds or more. The motorhome is overloaded before it leaves the driveway.

The situation is better with Class A motorhomes, right? I can be sure I've got plenty of payload if I spend more money, can't I? Please say yes.

Sorry. One popular 40-foot model figures out to have 1,680 pounds left for people and other essentials. Add the customary generator, forget or find it inconvenient to empty the holding tanks, and someone is likely to have to be shipped home by UPS. The list price is $79,941. By planning carefully, you could probably stay within the limits. Just don't let little Angus add too many rocks to his collection.

Another example is a 34-foot Class A listing for $79,500. With a listed payload of 2,000 pounds, it has 90 gallons of fuel, 100 gallons of fresh water, 35 gallons of propane, plus 6 gallons of water in the water heater. That leaves about 300 pounds for the family and essentials. With most families I've seen, that motorhome is overloaded before you leave the driveway.

Spend more money and get more safety, huh? Well, let's see. Here's a beautiful basement model 33-footer for $105,000. It lists a GVWR of 16,000 pounds and a dry weight of 14,000 pounds. With full tanks, it has 500 pounds left for such things as you and your food and clothing. I suppose you could seal the basement storage areas and fill them with helium. They certainly wouldn't be good for much else.

To be fair, there are lots of motorhomes, both Class A and Class C, with adequate to ample payloads. Some can carry as much as 10,000 pounds before hitting the GVWR. The point is, shouldn't we expect that manufacturers would build rigs with adequate capacity for the job they seem to be intended to do?

I mentioned earlier that weight distribution is important, too. An owner wrote that his Class C was a bit "squirrely" on the road. When he weighed it he found that the rear axle alone was carrying 10,500 pounds with an axle rating of 8,000 pounds. The GVWR for the motorhome was 11,500 pounds. With the normal weight in front -- I suppose the rig has an engine -- he was seriously overloaded. More importantly, the rear axle load was dangerous. With the normal extreme rear overhang of Class C motorhomes, the front end was so light that steering was difficult. How would you like to negotiate Wolf Creek Pass in that rig? What could he do to improve matters? Not much. How can you take 2,000 pounds out of a motorhome?

A friend told me his son was watching a Class C at a stoplight. The driver wanted to make a right turn. When traffic cleared, he gunned the motorhome -- and did a "wheely." The front end would not come down until the driver applied the brakes. Climbing a mountain grade in that rig would have to qualify as one of life's most interesting experiences.

With a few exceptions, the situation is not as bad with travel trailers and fifth-wheels. Most give more than enough payload for average needs. But it is not impossible to find such things as a 32-foot trailer with only 1,200 pounds of payload. Remember, though, that the only time the trailer will hold passengers is when it is parked. The payload need only include such things as water, propane, food, clothing and personal items. Even these can crowd the limits when the trailer is used for extended trips or full-timing.

Last January at the Tampa Super Show, I overheard a shopper ask a manufacturer of a Class C motorhome what the rear axle rating of his motorhome was. The reply was, "You're getting technical, Bud. I just buy a frame and slap a box on it."

The lesson is clear. Some manufacturers will be happy to take your money for a rig that is unsafe at any speed. Some will continue to build rigs with inadequate carrying capacity. Such behavior invites intervention by governmental agencies intent on protecting our interests. It would be much better if the industry would police itself. Until that time, look carefully at the GVWR and dry weight of any RV you're interested in buying. Know something about the weight ratings of the chassis used. Be certain there is sufficient carrying capacity for the load you want to carry. Then, remember that it is possible to overload any RV if you don't keep a sharp eye on Angus and his rocks.

Chapter 34

Wind Deflectors For Fuel Economy

A recent study by Peterbilt Motors, the big truck manufacturer, found some things that might be interesting to RVers looking for better fuel mileage. The study showed that significant savings could be made by minor modifications to the equipment and driving practices. Some of them are directly applicable to RVs. An earlier chapter dealt with some of these findings.

We RVers spend a lot of money on fuel for our thirsty beasts. I don't want to depress you, but only about 40% of the energy in the fuel our engines burn is used to develop power. The rest goes out the exhaust pipe or is dissipated as heat. That's not a pretty picture. There isn't much we can do about the heat losses, and we can't reduce the exhaust losses very much. But we can affect the way the 40% that goes into engine power is used.

Of the 40% that moves our rigs down the road, 40% is used to overcome aerodynamic drag. There are ways we can cut the drag. Aerodynamic drag depends on total frontal area, shape of the vehicle and speed. Frontal area is simply the width of the vehicle multiplied by its height. If your RV is 8 feet wide and 9 feet high, it has a frontal area of 72 square feet. That's easy to figure for a motorhome but not so easy for a trailer and tow vehicle.

It would seem that since the tow vehicle is both more narrow and lower in height than the trailer, it would only be necessary to consider the frontal area of the trailer. Not so. Look from the side view at a typical car towing a trailer. The car displaces the air as it passes through. The air tries to follow the contour of the car.

MEASURE FRONTAL AREA

As a result, the air comes down over the rear of the car. That means that the total frontal area includes the cross section of the car at its widest point plus the frontal area of the trailer. If the car is 5 feet wide by 5 feet high and the trailer is 8 feet by 9 feet, the total frontal area is 25 square feet + 72 square feet or 97 square feet.

The second factor in aerodynamic drag is shape of the vehicle. Flat shapes faced square to the direction of motion create lots of drag. Turn the plate at an angle and the drag is less. That's one reason engineers put round corners and sloping surfaces on cars. That's also where wind deflectors come into the picture.

Wind deflectors do two things when they are designed right. They lessen the amount of total frontal area, and they modify the shape. Total frontal area can be decreased if the deflector is designed and positioned so that the air coming off of it flows over the top of the following surface rather smashing into the front of the surface. That means the deflector must be as large as practical and positioned as far back on the tow vehicle as possible. The ideal would be for the deflector to be as wide as the tow vehicle, reach to the top of the trailer and have the top edge within inches of the front of the trailer.

Obviously, not all of that is possible. Failure to come close to those design requirements is the reason many deflectors accomplish little or nothing. Peterbilt found that a properly designed and positioned deflector can save nearly 7% of your fuel bill.

SPEED CRITICALLY IMPORTANT

The third factor in aerodynamics is speed, and it may be the most important. As far as aerodynamic drag is concerned, it makes little difference what your road speed is. Air speed is vitally important. To illustrate, to double the air speed requires eight times the power. If it takes one gallon of fuel to overcome the air drag of a forty miles per hour wind, it would take eight gallons to overcome an eighty miles per hour wind.

So what? you say. I'm not going to drive my RV 80 miles per hour. I'm glad, but let's look at some speeds you might consider. The difference between 50 mph and 60 mph may not seem like much. That is only a 20% increase. But driving at a 60 mph air speed requires nearly 175% the fuel required at 50 mph. If your rig gets 10 mpg at 50 mph it will get only about 6.8 mpg at 60 mph. That's a significant difference and worth considering.

To sum all of this up, here are some things you can do. Drive at a reasonable speed. As a rule of thumb, for each mph over 55 that you drive, fuel requirements increase by 1.5% to 2.5%. That difference includes the increased aerodynamic drag and the increased friction at higher speeds.

Use a wind deflector with trailers. Deflectors work best with vans, station wagons and pickups with caps on the bed. Use a large deflector positioned at the extreme rear of the tow vehicle.

THINK AERODYNAMICS

Improve the aerodynamic shape of your rig. Using a wind deflector helps here, too. So does removing unnecessary things that stick out in the breeze. Over-large mirrors exert more drag than you would expect. So do extra mirrors. Baggage pods on top of the tow vehicle or roof of the RV cost fuel.

Think aerodynamics when you buy your next RV.

Class C motorhomes and pickup campers have terrible aerodynamic shapes. The air comes up over the hood, is deflected by the windshield and then gets trapped by the cabover. The turbulence is terrific. Turbulence represents wasted fuel. Fifth-wheel trailers also operate at an aerodynamic disadvantage with their extra frontal area. I like fivers but those with rearward sloping front surfaces reduce the drag. Fivers with stand-up front rooms like the one I own have an extra 12 square feet of frontal area.

Rounded edges and corners lessen the drag. The rounded surfaces on Airstreams and similar trailers are the big reason they tow with less fuel than boxier trailers. But the advantage of rounded corners can be had with less extreme contours than Airstream has used. Even gently rounded edges are better than square ones.

Decrease the exit turbulence. Nothing was said about this factor earlier, but it is important. Look at the back of your rig after driving all day on a wet, sloppy highway or traveling down a dusty road. That dirt is on the rear end because of bad aerodynamic design. The air flows over the top and past the sides smoothly until it gets to the end of the rig. There it meets with a low pressure area just behind the RV. The air tries to fill that low pressure area but can't turn quickly enough. The result is turbulence, lots of it, and lots of drag.

You can remedy the situation, lower your fuel bill and get a cleaner rig by installing a different type of deflector at the rear. What is needed is something like the rear deflectors found on some station wagons. Placing one at the rear, top edge would help. So would placing one vertically at each rear, side edge. Using all three would be best of all.

Peterbilt's study showed that the modifications suggested here will pay for themselves in average use. But even if you don't want to spend the money to make the modifications, you can save fuel dollars without spending an extra cent.

Slow down. Just say, "No, I won't go 65."

Chapter 35

Winterizing Your RV

I used to hate the term "winterize." It represented everything I disliked about RVing, plus it was an irritating job. There was something about having to say, "This is an end of camping for the season, Buster" that was almost more than I could take. I put it off as long as possible. To be honest, sometimes I had to light the furnace to thaw the water pipes so that I could drain them. I'll bet I'm not the only one who has done that.

Winterizing is no longer an irritating job, but I still hate to see the end of an RVing season. That's what I and millions of others get for living where the year is eight months of tundra and four months of tough sledding.

But you don't want to hear about my dislikes. You started reading to find out how to prepare your rig for the winter, so I had better get to it.

Fortunately, winterizing is a lot easier today than it was 30 years ago. Now we have special anti-freeze for RVs and a gadget called a water heater by-pass. These two have made life much easier.

FIRST THE WATER TANK

Start by draining the water tank. If you don't know where the drain valve is, look in your owner's manual. Usually the drain valve is located on the side wall of the RV near the tank filler. While the tank is draining, drain

the water heater. There is a drain plug located near the bottom of the heater inside the access door. The plug may be a removable plastic plug, or the plastic plug may have been replaced by a valve. Open it and let the tank drain. Opening a hot water faucet at the opposite end of the RV will facilitate draining the water heater.

After the water heater has emptied, drain the water lines. On most RVs, there is a valve in both the hot and cold water lines, often behind one of the lower cabinets near the galley. If you can't find them, check your owner's manual. If you still need help, look under the rig for two small tubes hanging down close together. They will be about a half inch in diameter. In the cupboard directly above those drains will be the valves. Opening all faucets will speed up draining the water lines.

Some owners complete the process of winterizing the water system by blowing the remaining bits of moisture out with compressed air. I used to do that with simple systems, but I was always a little uneasy about the results. Now we have special, non-toxic anti-freeze for RVs. The idea is to fill all water lines with anti-freeze and stop worrying.

BY-PASS WATER HEATER

There are several ways to accomplish the result. If you dump the anti-freeze in the water tank, you can use the system water pump to circulate it through the pipes. You can also buy a gadget that inserts in the line between the water tank and the pump. The gadget has a siphon line that draws from the anti-freeze jug rather than the water tank.

In either case, unless you by-pass the water heater, you have to fill the water heater with anti-freeze before you can pump any anti-freeze through the hot water lines. That takes at least six gallons of anti-freeze before you get any in the water lines. That's expensive. A better way is to buy a by-pass kit from any RV dealer or parts supplier and install it on the water heater. The instructions are simple, and the kit is less expensive than six gallons of anti-freeze.

When the water tank and water heater have completely drained, close their drain valves and the drain valves on the water lines. Set the valves on the by-pass kit to by-pass the water heater. Pour a gallon and a half of anti-freeze in the water tank. Turn on the water pump and open the faucets farthest from the pump. Let the faucet run until the stream is bright red. Close the faucet and repeat with each faucet. Be sure to flush the toilet until it also runs bright red. On a large RV, you may need another gallon of anti-freeze to complete the job. Pour at least a cupful of the remaining anti-freeze in each drain. Now all the water lines, the water pump and all the drains should be protected from freezing. Turn off the water pump. If you have any anti-freeze left, pour it into the toilet and open the flush valve.

Remove the battery from your trailer or the house battery from your motorhome. Fill all cells to the proper level with distilled water. Hook the battery to a good charger overnight. Store batteries in the basement or someplace where they will not freeze. Every couple of months during storage, hook the batteries to the charger and give them an overnight trickle charge. The useful life of batteries that are permitted to sit in a partially discharged condition will be seriously shortened.

KEEP OUT UNWANTED GUESTS

Tape a piece of plastic over all vents and openings in the RV to keep out unwanted winter guests. You may find it to be an excellent idea to crawl underneath your RV with an aerosol can of foam. Any openings, however small, should be sprayed shut. Unless you have served as unwitting host to a family of mice in your RV, you won't believe what a small opening can serve as a mouse expressway. You won't believe the damage they can do, either.

Coat the battery terminals and the open ends of electrical plugs with some sort of anti-corrosion compound. Spraying with WD-40 is helpful. I like to tie a plastic bag over the trailer electrical plug and place the open end of the bag down so that any moisture that condenses will drain out. If you remove your propane tanks, also cover the open ends of the gas lines with plastic bags. Be sure to plug the open ends of the valves on the propane bottles.

Choose your winter storage location with care. You don't want to park under any limbs that might come down in a winter storm and make new ventilation openings in the roof. I also don't like to park on a lot that has tall weeds under the RV. Weeds often hide the nests of unwanted insects and mice. I like to park my RV so that each tire is on a block of wood with the RV level.

The tires should be protected from sunlight with some sort of shade. Pieces of plywood or snap-on covers of canvas or other material are satisfactory. Tires left exposed to sunlight and ozone are subject to sidewall cracking. Why doesn't it happen when the RV is in use? The tire manufacturers use a small amount of protective compound in the rubber. As the tire flexes the compound is released and protects the tire. But if the tire sits without exercise, the compound is not released. Shade your tires. Many astute RVers even cover their tires if they are going to be parked a couple of days.

PROTECT ENGINE, DRIVETRAIN

If you have a motorhome, winterizing gets a bit more involved. You have an expensive engine and drivetrain that need winter protection. Start by warming up the engine and then changing the oil and oil filter. Engine oils collect a variety of corrosive compounds as the result of fuel combustion. Those compounds, if left in the crankcase and bearings for the winter, can do a lot of damage. Change the oil and refill with your usual good grade.

If the motorhome is going to be driven during the winter, select a grade of engine oil appropriate to the temperatures where you will be traveling. Follow the advice in your owner's handbook. If the handbook is missing, select a good quality oil in 10W-30 weight rated SG for gasoline engines or CD for diesels.

While you're in the filter changing mode, change the oil and filter on your generator and change the air filter on your main engine. Service the air filter on the generator, too. Clean out any visible debris around the generator, and clean the grills over ventilation openings.

If you have a diesel engine, this is a good time to drain the water separator and add some fuel conditioner to the fuel tank. There is a fungus that seems to love diesel fuel. Unless you want to replace the fuel tank next spring, add some conditioner before storage.

INSPECT HOSES, CLAMPS

Inspect radiator and heater hoses and clamps. Check hoses for cracking by bending the hose. Squeeze the hoses to check for softness due to interior deterioration. Replace any hoses that show signs of checking, softness, or unusual swelling around hose clamps. Use new clamps of the type that have a threaded screw that fits in matching threads cut in the clamp material. After installing new hoses and clamps, check for signs of leaking and tighten a bit more.

Check all engine belts. Replace any that show signs of cracking or have worn, frayed edges.

Now is the time to drain the cooling system. Before refilling, the cooling system should be backflushed to remove as much sediment as possible. You can buy a backflushing kit at any parts store or auto department of variety stores. It installs easily in one of the heater hoses and attaches to a garden hose for backflushing. Just follow the simple instructions.

After the cooling system is clean, drain the water out. You may have to loosen the bottom radiator hose to get all of the water out. Check your owner's manual to determine the cooling system capacity. Pour in enough new anti-freeze to make a 50% solution. Finish filling with water. Start the engine and let it idle. Keep adding water until the level stabilizes. Replace the cap and continue running the engine until it is warmed up. Fill the radiator overflow tank nearly full with 50% anti-freeze/water solution. Remember next spring or whenever you place the motorhome in service to check the coolant level in the overflow tank and replenish as needed with 50% solution. A 50% solution gives maximum protection against corrosion and boiling and protects against freezing down to -34F.

REMEMBER TO LUBRICATE

Before storage, the chassis and driveshaft should be lubricated. It's an easy job that you can get satisfaction from doing and save yourself a few bucks. A hand-operated grease gun and grease cartridge can be purchased at the same store where you bought the backflush kit. Slide under the front of the motorhome -- take an old rag with you -- and look at the wheels and front axle. There will be a rod called a tie rod running from one wheel to the other. Each end will have a grease fitting. After wiping the dirt off the end of the fitting, fill each fitting until grease begins to run out of the joint.

Look for other similar rods and grease fittings and give them the same treatment.

The pivot points for the wheels as they turn for steering also need to be lubricated. Ford and most Dodges use kingpins. There should be a grease fitting at the top and bottom of each kingpin. Most GMC and Chevys use ball joints. To properly lubricate these fittings, you need to jack each wheel up until it hangs free and then, using your grease gun, fill the joint until grease begins to ooze out.

There will be two or more sets of universal joints on the driveshaft. Most of these will have grease fittings. Some have no fittings but were "permanently" greased when they were fabricated. If you are lucky enough to have universals with grease fittings, use your grease gun again. You may have to move the motorhome slightly to rotate the fittings around so that you can reach them. There will also be at least one slip fitting on the driveshaft. There will be a grease fitting. Use it.

If you see other grease fittings -- by now you know what they look like and have some notion of where they might be -- use your grease gun.

FILL THE FUEL TANKS

Drive your motorhome over to your favorite gas station and fill the fuel tanks. Leaving a partially filled tank sit around for several weeks is an invitation for the moisture in the air to condense in your tank. That means water in the bottom of the fuel tanks. Water causes the tank to rust out prematurely and wreaks havoc when it finds its way into the carburetor or injection system. It can also cause gas line freeze up if you drive the motorhome in the winter.

Back home, if you're parking the rig for the winter, drive it up on boards and place covers over the tires. Remove the battery and give it the same treatment mentioned earlier.

Sounds like a lot of work? It isn't really. But your RV cost a lot of money. If you protect it with proper winterizing, it will be much easier to get it ready for the next camping season, and it will last a lot longer before it needs expensive repairs.

Chapter 36

21 More Things Your Dealer Didn't Tell You

1. RIGHT HEIGHT

Hitching up a fifth-wheel trailer requires getting the hitch pin at the right height before backing the tow vehicle under it. You can speed up the process if you use a little trick. Assemble a piece of heavy cord -- chalk line will do -- with a heavy fishing sinker on one end. On the other end, fabricate some sort of adjustable hook. I made mine from a scrap of aluminum tubing off an old TV antenna. When you unhitch, measure the height of the pin above the ground before leveling. Adjust your cord and string to that height. When you're ready to hitch up next time, put your cord device in place and adjust the pin to that height. It will be very close and will save a lot of cussing and other strange antics.

2. TOILET TISSUE CHECKER

Why bother? you ask. Well, because some tissue doesn't break up into fibers very well. That kind tends to clog holding tanks and place an extra load on the dumping stations we use. Toss a couple sheets of the tissue you have into a clean pint jar. An empty mayonnaise jar works well. Fill the jar with water, replace the lid and shake vigorously for a couple of minutes. The paper should be reduced to tiny particles. I've found most toilet tissue made from recycled paper works well and it saves resources.

3. VISE DEVICE

If you're one of us who likes to carry a vise along to help with repairs, you've probably muddled through several ways of holding the vise in place while you use it. One owner I met bolts the vise to the inside surface of the tailgate on his truck. When the tailgate is opened, the vise is on a secure surface. When the tailgate is closed, the vise is stored out of the way where it won't rattle around. If you don't use a pickup, you can bolt the vise to a piece of 2 X 8 board about three feet long. The plank can be held to a picnic table with a couple of large C-clamps.

4. QUICK JUNCTIONS

If you are smart and use a water filter on your hose to the RV, you've probably cussed all the connections. Buy a couple sets of quick disconnects at a hardware store. Problem solved. If the water connection on your RV has enough space, you can use another quick disconnect there to speed things even more.

5. TANK FILLER

Filling the RV water tank can be a pain. The end of the hose won't stay in place unless you hold it, and the process seems to take forever. Buy a piece of half-inch clear plastic hose about 15 inches long or get a clean scrap of garden hose the same length. Fasten a female hose repair end to it. Attach the short hose to your water hose and stick it into the filler opening. The tank will fill faster without burping, and you can file your nails or kick the cat while the tank fills.

6. MAGIC PUTTY

No, not the stuff the kids play with. I'm talking about the putty tapes used at all the windows and doors and other openings on your RV. A dab of the stuff is great to hold things in place without staining the surface of counters or walls. Place a bit under anything you want to stay on a counter top while you drive. Hold small pictures to walls with some of the gooey stuff.

7. GET ORGANIZED

I carry lots of books in my RV. Some of them are stored in overhead compartments. In the old days, by the time I pulled from a campsite to the dump station, they were all rearranged. Then a friend showed me the error of my ways. Find heavy corrugated board boxes. Cut to the right height and width. Cut the ends on a diagonal from top rear to bottom front. Place the boxes in the compartment and load with books. They still move around a bit, but not so far that I can't find them. Stuffing extra bedding or towels in front of them when traveling would help even more.

8. PRESSURIZE

Not long ago, I stopped to help an RVer with a flat tire. Sure enough, the spare was also flat. That should give you a hint to check ALL tires, not just the ones on the ground. But, wouldn't it be nice to have a pump so that you could bring all tires up to the desired pressure before you leave camp? And if a tire loses air while you're driving, you might be able to pump it up enough to continue on to a repair station. That is, if you had a pump.

A hand pump works if you do. Better is one that runs off the battery in your RV. Most are slow but easier on the old heart than a hand pump. Make sure the one you get is capable of the pressures your tires need.

9 CHOCK IT

Think back over some of the places you've camped. What would have happened if the rig had rolled? Bye-bye. What you need is a set of wheel chocks. Sure, you can use rocks, but who wants to look that unprofessional? You can buy a fancy chock from your friendly RV dealer or you can make a set from wood blocks. If you make your own, they should be at least four inches high and six inches wide. Place them in front of and behind a single wheel or place one large block between tandem wheels.

Sometimes we forget to chock the wheels when we stop at a rest area or to go seeing the sights. I've parked in a lot of such places that were very steep. Relying on the "park" position in the transmission is placing a lot of trust in a small and brittle piece of metal. Take a moment to chock it and be safe.

10 MUSCULAR POWER CORDS

Why do so many campground owners place the outlet post 35 feet from an RV equipped with a 25-foot power cord? Oh well, just use this itsy bitsy extension cord here and everything will be okay. Not so. Our RVs use a lot of electrical power when we operate such things as air conditioners and microwave ovens. Even coffee makers and toasters are heavy current users. The lights and power converter alone use more current than a lightweight extension cord can safely handle. Feel them; they get warm. Then they get hot. And then they burn. Your extensions should be made from 10-3 wire with molded ends to keep out the moisture. I like to have two extensions, each 25 feet long. They are easy to handle, and I don't have to use a 50-foot extension when all I need is a short one.

11 HEADACHE STICK

I know a petite, silver-haired gypsy who has a hefty piece of shovel handle lying beside her RV door. I don't think it's for me, but I'll bet you that anyone who saw her greet them with her headache stick in hand would give serious thought to an appointment somewhere else. I also know another RVer who has a machete handy. My favorite stick is made of steel tubing and has a nice piece of walnut attached. Hold it just right, and it makes a loud noise guaranteed to get everyone's attention.

Let's face the facts: Not everyone found in a campground has your best interests at heart. Each of us has to decide how to handle the possible problem of unwanted callers. I've made mine.

12. BUNGEE, BUNGEE

I get letters from lots of RVers. Some are from motorhomers towing small vehicles with all wheels on the ground. Some of them complain that once in a while the front wheels of the towed vehicle don't recover properly on quick, sharp turns. The result is pounds of tire rubber being torn off. Most of the time, the cure is as simple as attaching a couple of pieces of bungee cord from the steering wheel to something solid so that the cord will help pull the wheel back into a straight-ahead position.

13. SCRUB-A-DUB

Face another fact. Not all campgrounds have nice, paved pads in front of our doors. Some seem to arrange for piles of sand and dirt. Sand and dirt usually aren't well liked by the person in charge of housekeeping chores. Find some way of removing dirt from shoes before entering the RV. One of the best is a device with brushes along the bottom and sides. A quick pass with each shoe removes most of the dirt. The person in charge of housekeeping chores stays in a good mood, and you get to continue eating there. There might even be other privileges. Get the gadget from your RV dealer.

14. IT'S NOT MY FAULT

Ever grab the door knob on your RV and feel an electric tingle run through your bod? No? Well, I have, and I'm here to tell you it will get your attention. It should never happen if you use the polarity checker mentioned in the first chapter. But to be really safe, I've turned my entire rig into a ground fault interrupter circuit. You know that funny looking outlet in the bathroom? If anything plugged into that outlet should feed an electrical current into you, the circuit will break so fast that you probably will never feel it. Now my whole RV works the same way. The ground fault interrupter circuit looks like a long pigtail adapter. It's installed between the power cord and the park outlet box. If a short circuit should ever develop in the rig's wiring and I should touch the rig while my feet are on the ground, the circuit will instantly break. I won't feel it, and I'll still be alive to fix the problem. Get it at your favorite RV dealership.

15. WALKIE TALKIE

A favorite source of entertainment in campgrounds is to watch newcomers trying to park. One is outside yelling and swinging arms in secret semaphore. The other is inside trying to respond. Great entertainment. Not so great a way to start the weekend.

Things work much better if you get a cheap hand-held CB. The partner in charge of directions talks softly into the CB. The driver listens on the CB in the rig. No swearing and no sweat. Buy the hand-held at your local Radio Shack for under $30. It needs only one channel and very low power.

16. HELP, I'M BLEEDING!

Where is your first-aid kit and what's in it? Don't know? It's not much good, then, is it? Every rig should have a first-aid kit. People do get hurt. Sometimes, they can't wait while someone else drives them 50 miles to a clinic or hospital. Some first-aid kits are much more complete than others, but any kit is better than none. Get the best you know how to use.

How long has it been since you had a first-aid course? That long, huh? Is the life of your partner worth spending a couple of evenings learning what to do in an emergency? Change the question. Is your life worth having your partner spend a couple of evenings learning how to save your worthless hide? Check around. In almost every community there is someone ready, willing and qualified to teach first aid. While both of you take the course, you should also learn the latest cardio-pulmonary resuscitation techniques. If you ever have a heart attack, I'm certain you would like to have someone nearby who knows how to keep you alive until the medics get there.

17. GET RID OF THE WEIGHT

Every pound of stuff you carry around costs just a little more in fuel consumed. Each year your RV should go on a reducing diet. Take everything out. If you didn't use it during the last year, get rid of it. The odds are you won't use it this year or next. Get rid of it. Then you can start accumulating more junk to throw away next year.

18. CARPET CLEANERS

Well, carpets for cleaning. Small rugs in high-traffic areas can make it much easier to keep the place clean and cut down on wear to the permanent carpeting and linoleum. Some people like throw rugs. Others have found that carpet samples that are being thrown away at carpet stores are better and cheaper. Think of all the places you could use one and then go ask for them. They also make great pads for folding metal chairs. (And, adds my editor, great ground cloths for emergency under-the-rig repairs.)

19. HOBO WASHER

Not to wash your favorite hobo, but to wash his clothes. Got a few duds that need to be made civilized but you're not ready for the big trip to the coin laundry? Put them in a plastic bucket with a tight lid, add water and a bit of detergent. Cover securely and drive to the next campground. The clothes will be clean. All you have to do is rinse them and hang them out to dry.

20. AUTOMATIC DRYER

There are so many ways to make portable clothes dryers that I can't possibly mention them all. Retractable lines are fine. So is a hank of rope or heavy cord stretched between two convenient trees. There are folding gadgets made of wood dowels that expand to give drying space. A large embroidery hoop with clothes pins attached around the edge and suspended by cords works well. Suit yourself.

21. ZIP IT

Okay, okay, but I had to close this book with something starting with the letter Z, and Velcro comes close to being a zipper. It's great for attaching almost anything to a wall or a carpet. I've got a tall, slender basket in the bathroom. It looks nice but would fall over and scatter whatever it has accumulated as soon as I pull out of the campsite. It also stands on a trap door in the floor. A couple of pieces of Velcro solved the problem. Rubber cement holds one piece to the basket and the mating part to the wall. Bingo, the basket stays in place, and I can easily remove it to get at the trap door storage space in the floor just below.

TRY THESE COMPANION BOOKS

Guide to Free Campgrounds

Sixth Edition

by Don Wright

560 pages
$12.95 (including postage)
$23.90 with Guide to Free Attractions
$32.90 Value Pack
includes Save-A-Buck Camping

This 1990-91 updated guide to thousands of free U.S. campgrounds lists cost-free locations alphabetically by state and city. It provides detailed directions to each campground as well as information on the facilities and activities available. Because of their non-commercial nature, most of the campgrounds are located in beautiful, natural settings. Author Don Wright is America's leading authority on camping and the RV lifestyle. He has camped virtually everywhere in the U.S.

Guide to Free Attractions

Fifth Edition

by Don Wright

640 pages
$12.95 (including postage)
$23.90 with Guide to Free Campgrounds
$32.90 Value Pack
includes Save-A-Buck Camping

Ghost towns, gold mines, caves, museums, zoos, historical sites, natural wonders, tours, exhibits. They're all listed in this newly updated guide to 6,000 of the best free attractions in the U.S. Including more than 2,000 newly listed attractions, this popular book also lists wineries, battle sites, art centers, covered bridges, public gardens, restored homes, historic cemeteries, waterfalls and fish hatcheries.